TO:

_____

FROM:

_____

DATE:

_____

Moments
of Grace
— FOR WOMEN —

Stories & Scriptures to Warm
Your Heart & Refresh Your Soul

Carol Kent, General Editor
and Thelma Wells

Christian Art
PUBLISHERS

Visit Christian Art Gifts, Inc., at www.christianartgifts.com.

Moments of Grace for Women: Stories & Scriptures to Warm Your Heart & Refresh Your Soul

Previously published by Zondervan as *Kisses of Sunshine for Women*. Copyright © 2005. Revised and updated in 2025 by Carol Kent and Ellie Kay.

Published by Christian Art Gifts, Inc., IL, USA.

First edition 2025.

Designed by Christian Art Gifts, Inc.

Cover and interior images used under license from Shutterstock.com.

Most Christian Art titles may be purchased at bulk discounts by churches, nonprofits, and corporations. For more information, please email SpecialMarkets@cagifts.com.

ISBN 978-1-63952-896-7

Printed in China.

30 29 28 27 26 25
10 9 8 7 6 5 4 3 2 1

To my granddaughters and my great granddaughter:

Vanessa C. Wells

Alaya L. Cohen

Alyssa E. Wells

Bryna A. Cohen

Auriana M. Cox

– Thelma Wells –

To women who make a positive difference in my life:

Anne Denmark

Cathy Gallagher

Janet Fleck

Ginger Shaw

Kathe Wunnenberg

– Carol Kent –

Other Books in the Moments of Grace Series

Moments of Grace for Moms
> By Carol Kent and Ellie Kay

Moments of Grace for Grandmas
> by Carol Kent and Gracie Malone

Moments of Grace for Sisters
> by Carol Kent

Moments of Grace for Teachers
> by Carol Kent and Vicki Caruana

Contents

Introduction

This series of five books—one each for women, moms, sisters, grandmas, and teachers—has lighthearted, uplifting, and often humorous stories meant to bring a sunburst of joy to your life as you remember that God loves you. Thelma Wells, beloved Women of Faith speaker and author, joined me in putting these stories together. Our purpose is simply to let God's love so warm and fill you that you become warmth, light, and love to a cold, dark world.

There's nothing quite as comforting as reading the stories of women who allow us to laugh out loud at their crazy antics, empathize with their imperfect choices, feel their hurts, celebrate their successes, and point us to the truth of God's Word. This book is for women of all ages who are interested in personal and spiritual growth.

Thelma's stories teach us how to embrace our worth in God. She brings us to an understanding of His role in erasing the baggage of shame and guilt we may be dragging around. She says we don't have to live with our guilt. Instead, we can give it to God because of what Jesus did on the cross.

Some of these stories will make you laugh out loud, and others will make you dry a tear. I pray that *Moments of Grace for Women* will nurture your soul as it leads you to fresh faith, renewed hope, and purposeful living. I also want to thank the remarkable women who shared their stories in this book. You inspired, motivated, and encouraged me—but most of all, you reminded me that my goal in life is not perfection. Your genuine authenticity will help every reader to be "the real deal" in her relationships with others.

Happy reading!
Carol Kent,
General Editor

He Knows My Name

— Thelma Wells —

The beginning of wisdom is to call things by their right names.

Chinese proverb

My mother was little more than a child herself when, at age seventeen, she gave birth to me. Not only was she young, she was crippled and unmarried. In scribbled handwriting, from the back room of my grandparents' home in Dallas, Texas, she wrote "Baby Girl Morris" on my birth certificate. However, she called me "Thelma" after the midwife who helped deliver me. Later I assumed the distinctive last name of "Smith" from my biological father.

It wasn't until I applied for a passport to take a trip to Panama that I encountered a real problem, when all I could produce was a birth certificate that read "Baby Girl Morris." I had to spend $175 in a court of law to buy the name I had used all my life.

Not many women can say, "I was a girl without a name," but I meet women every day who have no idea who they really are. It is one of the greatest privileges of my life to be able to say (and write a book with the title) *Girl, Have I Got Good News for You!*

The aspect of sharing God's love with women that I most enjoy is helping them regain their self-esteem. I get so excited as I am able to "midwife" them into an understanding of God's role in erasing the baggage of shame and guilt they may be dragging around. I tell them, "You don't have to live with silent, private guilt all of your life. What may have happened in your past is over and should be done with. It's history. You can pack your guilt and shame away in a box, use duct tape around the edges to seal it tightly, and put it in the trash where it belongs, because Jesus wants you to bring it to Him."

And after I have delivered this good news, I tell them they have a new name. They are not a nobody; they are not a generic Baby Girl Doe in their Father's eyes. He calls them by a holy name. They are blessed, redeemed, and precious. They are His lambs, daughters of the King, His bride.

I paid $175 for a piece of paper that says my name is Thelma Wells.

Jesus paid with His life, on a cross, to give me a new name written in the Book of Life. Today I happily and legally go by the earth name of Thelma, but I know my true identity. My heavenly name is Daughter of God, Beloved, and Forgiven.

"Fear not, for I have redeemed you;
I have called you by name,
you are mine."

ISAIAH 43:1 ESV

A Surprise in the Closet

– Shari Minke –

All that we send into the lives of others comes back into our own.

Edwin Markham

Ugh! I tried pushing the hangers in my bedroom closet. Curling my fingers behind the metal rod, I felt the obstacle preventing my success. I pulled out a wad—it was two crumpled ten-dollar bills! Instantly my fingers went into search mode feeling for more "wads." Ha! I discovered another one, then another, and another! Laughter bubbled out of me as I threw money on the floor. I dropped to the floor, flattened the money, and counted.

I rushed over to the phone and called my husband. "You'll never guess what just happened! I found $800 in our closet!"

Tom was as stunned as I was.

"What do we do with the money?" I asked.

Tom chuckled. "Call your dad—he's a wise man—but the first thing I want you to do is to check *all* the closets!"

Finding no more money, I called my father. Dad's counsel

was this: "According to the law, when you purchase a house, all its contents become your property, so legally the money is yours. But you have to ask yourself, 'What is the *ethical* thing to do?' Ask God. He will show you what He wants you to do with the money."

Seven years earlier we had purchased our home from a man named Fred. We learned that Fred built the home for his wife. It was their dream house. After they lived in the home for only two years, Fred's wife died of cancer. He left the house empty for another two years, unable to bear the thought of selling it.

During the seven years we had lived in the house, Fred passed away. Fred's daughter, Judy, lived in our subdivision. I struggled with whether the money should go to Judy.

I told God honestly, "I really want this money. You know it would help with our current cost of finishing the basement, but what do *You* want me to do with it? Please show me."

A few days later while reading my Bible, words on the page seemed to blaze like neon lights. "Keep your lives free from the love of money and *be content with what you have*" (Hebrews 13:5, my emphasis).

In that moment I had the answer. God also impressed on my heart this message: *Wait. I will tell you when to give Judy the money.*

The following Sunday I felt like I was hit with a bolt of lightning. God spoke to my heart, saying, *Go! Go now*! I jumped off the couch, stuffed the money in my pocket, and said to Tom, "I'm going to Judy's house!"

When Judy opened the door, I could see she had been crying. I asked if I could come in, and she graciously invited me inside.

"Judy, a couple of weeks ago while I was moving the clothes in my closet, I discovered some money hidden up under the rod."

Dropping her head, she smiled. "That would have been my mother."

I pulled the large wad of bills out of my pocket and said, "Well, this money belongs to you."

Judy sat stunned for a moment as I placed the bundle in her hands. Then she shook her head as if coming out of shock and said, "Uh, no, wait. You found the money—it belongs to you."

"No, Judy. The money belongs to *you*."

Tears streamed down her face. "I've been alone for a while. It's not often that my husband and kids are out at the same time. Just before you came over, I was missing my mother so badly I walked into the family room and took a picture of her off the wall. As I was holding the picture, I said aloud to God, 'Please, just let me know my mom is okay.' Then you showed up at the door."

Now both of us were crying!

For seven years I had shifted the seasonal clothes in my closet. Never had the hidden wads of money hindered me.

How inconceivable that God knew a day would come when Judy would be missing her mother so terribly and call out to Him for comfort. God was there, waiting to answer her call.

Two weeks later Judy and her husband showed up on our doorstep. Smiling, Judy handed me an envelope and said, "We feel you should have half of the money. You didn't have to tell us about finding it. We want to share the gift!"

Gratefully we received the money and used it to help remodel Judy's parents' dream house.

So in everything, do to others what
you would have them do to you.

MATTHEW 7:12

I Love Chocolate!

– Carol Kent –

God loves to use our bad habits to bring about His good.
Marnie Swedberg

I *love* chocolate. I've told my husband that when I die, I'd like to be dipped in chocolate and shipped off for burial in Hershey, Pennsylvania. I live in a house with another chocoholic, so I have a special hiding place for it. I keep some in the refrigerator. There's almost always some in the freezer. I keep a little in the Halloween treat candy jar on the top shelf of the cupboard. And a tin labeled Borwick's Baking Powder usually contains semisweet chocolate chips reserved for when it's time to fold them into the cookie dough, if they last that long.

I was home recently and had planned to spend the day working. After jumping out of bed, I donned a pair of old jeans and a faded, well-worn sweater. I hurriedly brushed my hair and didn't put on any makeup. (Even relatives might not have recognized me. My sister Paula has a make-up case with printing on the side that says, "My face is in this bag." I need that bag.)

Seated at my desk, I opened the Bible to Matthew 5, the text for my next retreat message, and began a careful reading of the Beatitudes. I came to verse 6 and read, "Blessed are those who hunger." What do you guess I thought about?

I went to the refrigerator—no chocolate! I tried the freezer—no chocolate. The Halloween treat candy jar, too, was empty. Instinctively, I went to the pantry and pulled out the Borwick's Baking Powder can, knowing I had purchased chocolate chips just the week before. I reached inside and pulled a note from the bottom of the can. "Sorry, honey, I beat you to it!"

I was disappointed. *Obviously, the Lord doesn't want me to have any chocolate this morning.* I reluctantly went back to my desk to concentrate on message preparation. After fifteen minutes I thought, *Why, it's only three miles to the store. I could be there and back in no time at all and satisfy this ridiculous craving.*

After making the decision to go to the store, I caught a glimpse of myself in the mirror. I didn't want to be seen looking this way. It took me at least half an hour to apply makeup and put on appropriate clothing. So when I got to the store, I decided to make the trip worth my while. I picked up the largest Hershey's bar with almonds I could find. Then I grabbed a giant-size Cadbury Caramello. (For those not into this sort of thing, this is chocolate and caramel in one mouthwatering bite!) On my way to the checkout, I picked up the biggest bag of M&M'S on the shelf.

As I walked out of the store and crossed the parking lot to my car, I consumed one-third of the Hershey's; on the three-mile trip home, I finished it off. I picked up the Cadbury. Thinking quickly, I realized that the M&M'S would taste terrific with a big pot of coffee. I envisioned a delightful study time, sipping coffee and eating M&M'S—one by one, all day. While the coffee in my drip pot worked its way to the bottom, I continued devouring the Cadbury. When I heard the final gurgle, signaling that the coffee was ready, I was just finishing off the very last bite of my second sixteen-ounce candy bar.

This was the moment I realized I was so sick I could hardly move.

I'm ashamed to admit it, but that day—a day I had reserved for Bible study, prayer, and preparation for ministry—I wasted hours of precious time over a ridiculous human craving. It wasn't the first time.

An important lesson was learned the hard way. A bad habit can be stopped by a better decision the next time temptation knocks on my door.

So if you're serious about living this
new resurrection life with Christ,
act like it. Pursue the things over which
Christ presides. Don't shuffle along,
eyes to the ground, absorbed with the things
right in front of you. Look up, and be
alert to what is going on around Christ ....
And that means killing off everything
connected with that way of death: ...
doing whatever you feel like whenever you
feel like it, and grabbing whatever attracts
your fancy. That's a life shaped by things
and feelings instead of by God.

COLOSSIANS 3:1–2, 5 MSG

The Lost Keys

– Jennie Afman Dimkoff –

Always ... set a high value on spontaneous kindness.
Samuel Johnson

"Bernie, will you go back to the van for more product?" I asked, handing her the keys. "We're already getting low on stock, and the crowd after the parade will be unbelievable."

I owned a small art business for fifteen years, and one of the best aspects of the work included exhibiting our wares at several upscale outdoor arts-and-crafts shows through-out the summer. One of my favorite events was the Coast Guard Festival held annually in Grand Haven, Michigan. With thousands of people pouring into the beautiful port city, the show was so busy I always had to hire extra staff. For this particular show, I had hired Bernadine to tend the booth with me. She was one of my dearest and most fun friends.

"I'll hold things down here while you're gone—but hurry, okay?" I added, feeling a bit overwhelmed at the thought of waiting on a line of customers without the aid of an assistant.

Bernie was gone for a *long* time. When she finally returned, my normally vivacious, fun-loving friend seemed subdued. After setting down my keys beside my briefcase, she quietly went about restocking the tables.

I watched Bernie, perplexed by my friend's unusual demeanor, and noticed a dark-blue stain on the edge of her right sleeve, which was rolled up high on her arm.

"Bernie, what in the world did you get on your blouse?"

A stricken look crossed her face. Yanking at the sleeve in question, she burst into tears. Words tumbled out on top of each other.

"Oh, Jennie, it was awful! On my way to the van, I passed a row of Porta Potties and figured it would be wise to make use of the facilities right then rather than after I was loaded down with product. So I did."

Bewildered by her distress, I nodded.

In great agitation, she continued with her story. "Well, just as I was turning to leave the cubicle, I heard something *awful*. It was the sound of your keys hitting the toilet seat! I stood there in shock for a moment, and then I opened the door to tell the people waiting that they simply *couldn't* go inside because I'd dropped my keys down the hole and had to get them back!"

She went on breathlessly. "A man from the line kindly went to his car and came back with a coat hanger, and I fished and I fished!"

My mind raced as I took in what my friend was saying.

"And finally," she went on anxiously, "in desperation, I held my breath and closed my eyes, and I reached down and *got* them! Then I raced to a gas station, and thank goodness there was hot water and soap! I scrubbed my hands and arm until my skin felt raw. And, Jennie, I swear I let scalding water run on your keys for at least ten minutes!"

As I stared at my friend in horror, two things became clear. First, her act of sacrifice for me was very likely *greater* than anything I could ever do in return. And second, it was best not to tell her I had a second set of keys in my purse.

Later, after the Coast Guard parade, various politicians who had taken part in the event circulated throughout the large art fair, meeting and greeting potential voters. The governor of Michigan stopped by our booth and warmly greeted each of us. After he left, Bernie turned to me with her first real smile of the afternoon.

"Well," she said with a grin while looking down at her right hand, "I figured it was best *not* to tell the governor where the hand he just shook had been earlier today."

Thinking back on that day, I marvel over having a friend who would go to such great lengths to help me. How could she have done what she did? Then I am reminded of Jesus Christ, the dearest of friends, who was willing to perform the most radical act of friendship for me. He suffered shame, scorn, and pain. And then He laid down His life.

Greater love has no one than this:
to lay down one's life for one's friends.

JOHN 15:13

Birth of a Friendship

— Cheryl Gochnauer —

Shared grief is half the sorrow, but
happiness when shared is doubled.

Unknown

Dismay blanketed the office as news spread from cubicle
to cubicle: the wife of one of our favorite coworkers had
just lost her baby.

Jack's workstation was silent, a darkened room with
shadows falling on family photos and his three-year-old
son's crayon masterpieces. As employees whispered, I
slipped into the bathroom and wiped empathetic tears
for his wife, Suzanne. I had miscarried the year before and
understood the grief of preempted parenting.

I also knew the frustration of fielding inane comments from people who mean to help but trample tender
hearts instead.

"It was God's will."

"You'll have more children."

"At least you weren't too far along."

These phrases had left me feeling even more bereft.

Like Suzanne, I had a preschooler at home to hug me, to smile, and to remind me of exactly what I had lost. So, though I'd never met Suzanne, I wrote this young Christian mother a letter saying all the things I wished someone had said to me.

Suzanne wrote back. Our friendship was instant and deep, a sisterly bond forged by common hurt and common belief in the One who shared our troubles. Over the following year, we spent lots of time together. We were a couple of modern-day Hannahs trying to catch God's attention, and eventually the giggles outweighed the tears. As we were about to discover, our Father was listening to every word.

"I'm going to have a baby!" Suzanne's bubbly voice danced over the phone line. I celebrated like I was the one who was pregnant.

A week later, I was.

"No way!" But there it was. The test strip was bright blue.

While Suzanne dove into preparations for her coming child, I held back. *What if something happens to this baby?*

But Suzanne would have none of this. As I had once prompted her, she pushed me toward the Giver of Life. My hesitation gave way to cautious optimism, then to joyful planning of my own.

One sunny September afternoon, Carrie Marie arrived, healthy and perfect. As I stood over the birthing room bassinet admiring her shining red hair, a familiar face appeared beside me.

"Hey, neighbor!" Jack beamed. "We're right next door!"

Within the hour, I was walking the hospital halls with Suzanne and Jack as my newborn slept. In true been-there, done-that fashion, I cheered Suzanne on as she waddled along, clutching her contracting belly. "You're gonna do great!"

And she did. A few hours later, I held Carrie to my breast and listened as Suzanne gave one last push in the adjoining birthing room. Garrett Neal squalled a robust hello as I laughed out loud and thanked God not only for His mercy but also for His impeccable timing.

A dozen years have passed since that glorious day when God filled both our arms with cherub-cheeked treasure. Suzanne and I now smile at our precocious preteens and their equally adored older siblings, keenly aware of how special they are—just like our other children, who are playing at Jesus' house until their mommies come home.

For the LORD is good and his love endures forever;
his faithfulness continues through all generations.

PSALM 100:5

30

Queen Bee
– Thelma Wells –

Don't even try to bury me
without my bumblebee pin!
Thelma Wells

When guests walk into the large sunroom in my home, they are often attacked by a swarm of bees. Not live bees, mind you, but plush bees, paper bees, toy bees, and ceramic bees. I have bee coffee mugs, bee paperweights, bee potholders, and my prize—a diamond bee brooch. I even own a bumble-bee toilet seat!

If there is an item with a bee attached to it, honey (no pun intended), I've probably bought it, received it as a gift, or created it.

Why this obsession with bees?

Years ago, I happened upon some startling informa-tion. I learned that the humble bumblebee is scientifically too big, its wingspan too narrow, for it to fly. Yet it buzz-es around anyway doing what God made it to do. Like the bumblebee, I didn't come into the world equipped to fly. As you've already learned, I began life with so many strikes against me that I should be a welfare statistic or hopelessly emotionally scarred.

But the miraculous power of God became the wind beneath this chubby little girl's wings and helped her learn to fly in spite of all that logic would dictate. I was born into poverty, but with God's grace I graduated from college and became a corporate speaker for the banking industry. I wasn't even given a legal name when I was born, but now I speak to thousands of women, telling them of their truest identity, and of a Father who has loved them from the moment they came into existence.

In the days of segregation, I learned what it was like to be hated and mistreated because of the color of my skin. I could have refused to associate with white people as a way to get my revenge.

My marriage suffered more than enough blows to have easily and almost predictably ended in divorce, but with God's amazing grace—and two wounded people willing to do the work of restoration—George and I have not only stayed married for forty years but we each still think the other is the cutest thing walking around on two legs.

I've survived nearly every heartbreak a mother can anticipate with a prodigal child, but today that prodigal is a productive citizen and loving parent. I don't mean to imply that all is perfect, for no relationships are without their faults. Life gives all of us continual challenges. But overall—oh my! God has been so good, so faithful to me.

I've been stuck on the floor of despair, with a heart that said, "I *cannot* get up again, Lord! I can't do this!"

But He won't let me stay on the floor. He says, "Thelma, of course you can't fly on your own. You have to soar on the wind of my Spirit. With my wind beneath those little wings of yours that are always flappin' in prayer, you will rise. Child, hold on. You and I, together, are about to fly above your circumstances."

Time and time and time again, He proved faithful when all seemed lost. In fact, I've learned to fly under so many impossible situations that I think I may now be qualified to be called a Queen Bee.

Do you feel as though you have fallen and simply cannot get up? Trust His power to change your life. Offer up a prayer of faith and believe your Father will take care of you and all of your concerns. Let go of the stuff that weighs you to earth. Embrace anything that lifts you higher. Soon you'll be off the dark ground of despair and buzzin' around in the fresh morning air.

God met me more than halfway,
he freed me from my anxious fears.
Look at him; give him your warmest smile.
Never hide your feelings from him.
When I was desperate, I called out,
and God got me out of a tight spot.

PSALM 34:4–6 MSG

Mystery Shoppers

– Bonnie Afman Emmorey –

*The mystery of life isn't a problem to solve,
but a reality to experience.*

Frank Herbert

I was an exasperated mom. My son Nathan was two years old, and Jordan was an infant. Life should have been perfect, but I was starting to feel like a crazy woman. It felt like my life revolved around feeding babies, changing diapers, and doing laundry.

Thank goodness for Chris! I'd met her two years earlier at a basketball game when our first sons were two weeks old. We connected! Although from vastly different backgrounds, we shared kindred spirits. Chris and I spent hours on the phone discussing everything from current events to silent husbands. I believe she saved my sanity.

We often met at the local grocery store and, after running our errands, ended up in the coffee shop, where we would kick back, relax, and talk. Chris was highly creative, and we often found ourselves trying to figure out what we could do to bring in extra money as stay-at-home moms.

As we lingered over coffee one afternoon, a vice president of our grocery store chain sat down with us to chat. We both knew him through our church, but his job offer took us completely by surprise. He was developing a new program for store evaluation and wondered if we'd be interested in part-time employment.

He wanted to hire us, two *obvious* housewives, to become "mystery shoppers." The grocery store chain would give us money to shop at their stores all over northern Michigan and *pay us* to evaluate the efficiency of store employees. It was every woman's dream job—being *paid* to shop! The fact that we had to give everything back didn't bother us a bit. I have always considered shopping my best sport, so this appeared a perfect match.

Chris and I set off on our first day filled with high expectations of great fun—but some surprises were in store for me. As a part of our job description, we were asked to be rude to salesclerks, try to use expired coupons, and sneak items out of the stores on the bottom rack of the shopping carts—without paying for them. Obviously, our *real* job was to write up reports following store visits about how well the employees were doing with catching crooks.

At the end of our first day, I went home exhausted from the stress of being so deceptive and dishonest. I'd never done anything like this before in my life. Chris had a blast, but I told my husband I didn't think I could continue. It was too difficult.

Ron reminded me I had made a commitment, and I should follow through with the assignment. I went back to work anticipating another difficult experience but was surprised to discover that by the third day I was having a ball seeing how much I could get away with at each store. And I was *good* at it!

The following Sunday we studied James 1:27, "Pure and undefiled religion before God and the Father is this: ... to keep oneself unspotted from the world" (NKJV).

An alarm went off in my head. I could see exactly what happened. I had been hired to do a job that, if I had been doing it for any other reason, would have been morally and legally wrong. Yes, at first I had found it difficult and was tempted to quit, but the more I did it, the easier it became. I even *enjoyed* it! I had allowed myself to touch the world, and my perspective had been altered. What a lesson! Chris and I had been having so much fun we almost missed the important admonition that what we had undertaken demanded personal integrity and accountability—to God and to each other.

Over the next few years, Chris and I continued to be mystery shoppers, even resorting to simple disguises if we thought anyone might recognize us. It gave us time away from the routine of kids, husbands, and housework, produced needed income, and was great fun. But I had a new perspective. God *would* hold me accountable, and I'd better guard my heart regarding matters of personal integrity.

"Real religion, the kind that passes muster before God the Father, is this: ... guard against corruption from the godless world."

JAMES 1:27 MSG

Binkies, Baggage, and the Billion-Dollar Question

— Sandi Banks —

Our love for people and our hope in Christ will put us in a position to point to Christ when asked about it.

John Fischer

I stepped off the airplane with baby Laura in my arms. Grandpa met us at the gate and offered to hold her while I went downstairs to the baggage claim area. I stood alone, waiting for my bags—just me—and holding the baby's pacifier. A flight attendant began staring, first at me, then at the Binky, then back at me. Finally, she leaned over and whispered, "Excuse me, miss. Is this your first flight?"

Actually, issuing pacifiers to airline passengers who need them is not such a bad idea. Those folks are easy to spot. Their hands clutch the armrests, their eyes stare at the air-sick bag, and their faces pale as the plane picks up speed along the runway. My heart goes out to those with a deathly fear of flying. Moreover, it goes out to those who have had that fear—and sat next to *me*.

Rather quickly, as a seasoned flier, I discern their plight. If I sense the least bit of receptivity, I try to help them during takeoff by distracting them or convincing them that airplanes are, indeed, the safest way to fly. If this doesn't work, I attempt to comfort them with up-to-date research on jet propulsion and physics facts that explain how the thrust, lift, drag, and weight properties make it nearly impossible for the plane *not* to fly.

No one has ever requested to sit by me a second time. So much for trying to be helpful!

I'll never forget the time I settled into the window seat with my Bible, my journal, and a prayer that went something like this: "Oh, Lord, this is *my* time with *You*. Please don't put anyone in this row. Just You and me, Lord, all the way. Okay?"

Sanctimoniously, I buckled in and opened to the Psalms. In my peripheral view, I noticed someone putting a bag into the overhead compartment and settling into the seat beside me. Curtly, I muttered under my breath, "Lord, I thought we had a deal. This is a mistake!"

Then I heard a soft, quivering voice. "Aren't you *scared* to fly?"

Instead of immediately dispensing my usual helpful hints, I was overcome with compassion for this young girl whose name, I soon learned, was Miriam. Her question led straight into my own faith story.

"Actually, Miriam, I used to be petrified of flying. I had an awful fear of death."

"And you aren't scared anymore? Wow. *What happened?*"

The billion-dollar question.

I began to simply share how I dreaded every Easter as a child and was probably the only kid in Denver to shed sad tears into her Easter basket. "Though my outside was festive, with a pretty dress and new patent leather shoes, my inside was a different story." I told her how I listened to the Easter message in church and stressed over Jesus' death so much I would mentally shut down before hearing the wonderful part about His resurrection.

"I was so focused on the *bad* news that I never heard the *good* news! Then one day I learned I could have a personal relationship with the risen Lord, and I no longer needed to fear death. I could actually look forward to spending eternity with Him!"

The conversation took an exciting, life-changing turn as God began doing His miraculous work in this young woman's heart. The plane landed. After we disembarked, Miriam eagerly gathered her entire family, glanced in my direction, and said, "Now tell them everything you told me!"

In the course of my ten-minute layover, I shared my best condensed version of the gospel message before reboarding the airplane.

I thought back to my pious prayer request for uninterrupted time with the Lord. Thankfully, He'd overruled.

Our disappointments and our interruptions are often divine appointments. I wonder how many opportunities I've missed because my own agenda got in the way. I'm learning that God has a grand purpose and a plan for me every day. Sometimes it involves putting my own scheduled activity aside, no matter how admirable it seems, in order to follow His agenda.

At any moment, someone may ask me the billion-dollar question. I hope I never miss an opportunity to give the priceless answer.

Always be prepared to give an answer to everyone who asks you to give the reason for the hope that you have.

I PETER 3:15

An Unexpected Opportunity

– Carol Kent –

You go nowhere by accident.

Rev. Richard Halverson

With my bags packed, I jumped into the car for the three-hour trip to a luncheon speaking engagement. The trip went smoothly, and I was energized by the dynamic, responsive group. Following the event, with spirits soaring, I thought, *Life doesn't get much better than this!*

Back in the car, I drove yet another hour to Lansing, Michigan, where I'd planned to spend the night with the woman who had been my best friend in high school. We anticipated an evening of food, fun, and catching up on our lives before I left for a women's conference in Ohio the next morning.

Because I usually bypassed downtown Lansing on trips across the state, I was unfamiliar with the traffic patterns within the city. My stress mounted as I traversed unknown streets, realizing that rush hour had begun. I stopped at a red light and was about to hit the accelerator when the light turned green, and my engine died.

Within seconds, impatient people were honking their horns—the light had turned, and they wanted to move *now*! I desperately attempted to start the car. Nothing happened. Angry drivers began making their way around my vehicle, mouthing words at me through the windows—and I could tell they were *not* quoting Bible verses!

I pleaded: "Lord, You are the God of miracles. You fed all those people with that little boy's lunch. Compared to the big stuff you've done, it would be a small thing for you to zap this engine and get my car moving again. Would You please get this car started?"

Again nothing happened. I began to realize this situation called for a different type of prayer. Placing my hands on the steering wheel with authority, I prayed loudly, "God, what are *You* going to do with *Your* car? You and I have a commitment in Ohio tomorrow! How will we get there?" I thought if I switched ownership to Him, He would feel more responsibility to get involved in helping solve my problem. Again I tried to start the car. The engine turned over, and the car ran just long enough to get me out of the intersection and into a side street where there was less traffic. No amount of begging or pleading with God seemed to make any difference to my stalled engine.

I called a dealership that could provide service, and before long a tow truck arrived. Much to my surprise, the driver was a woman—and she knew her business very well. She hoisted my car into place, and I jumped into the cab of the truck as she began driving toward the service garage. As we rode down the highway, I haltingly said, "I hope you don't mind if I ask. You're very skilled at what you do. How did you get into this line of work?"

Peering in my direction, she smiled. "To tell you the truth, I have a bachelor of arts degree in Russian literature and I'm working on a master's degree in theology right now." The shocked look on my face did not startle her. She continued, "At this time last year I was working overseas in a Communist country in underground evangelism."

With astonishment, I said, "You mean, *you're a Christian?*"

"Yeah! You too?"

"Yeah! Me too!"

As we talked, she told me it had been the most difficult year of her life. She was headed for the mission field, and her heart longed to be there. But she had university debts and needed to pay her bills before she went into full-time ministry. Becoming a wrecker driver was the fastest way she could make the necessary funds to take care of her obligations. But it was hard. She bore the brunt of malicious comments and snide remarks from people who thought a female tow truck driver was a joke.

We pulled into the driveway of the service garage, and I found myself giving comfort and encouragement to my wrecker driver. Her passion for God was obvious, but she was discouraged. We prayed out loud together in the cab of that truck, and I gave her a hug before we said goodbye.

As I stepped out of the service garage, I realized the home of my high school friend was located right across the street. I didn't even need to call a cab. I walked across the street, knocked on the door of my very surprised friend, and related the story of this unusual day.

Early the next morning I crossed the street, walked into the garage, and asked the service manager if they had discovered what was wrong with my car. He scratched his head as he responded, "Lady, we've taken your car through every kind of test we have, and there's nothing wrong with it. It runs just fine, and we have no idea why you had a problem with it yesterday."

As I drove to the Ohio conference, God spoke to my heart: "Carol, you are My ambassador. Yesterday I had a lonely, discouraged tow truck driver in Lansing, Michigan, who desperately needed to be reminded that I care about her and have a plan for her life beyond her present difficult circumstances. You had a little extra time, and I picked you to be the one to pray with her and give her a message of encouragement."

I thought back to the day before. I had been impatient. Angry. Upset with God. My carefully made plans were interrupted. My carefully planned schedule was altered by a situation that seemed beyond my control. I was mad at God for allowing my car to have problems when I was trying to do His work.

At that moment, I realized that almost every day I have

interruptions that are actually *God-appointments* in disguise. I wonder how many opportunities I've missed in the past because I only saw the interruption.

I am the Lord your God,
who teaches you what is best for you,
who directs you in the way you should go.
If only you had paid attention to my commands,
Your peace would have been like a river,
Your well-being like the waves of the sea.

ISAIAH 48:17–18

The Color of Love

— Thelma Wells —

God loves you simply because He has chosen to do so. He loves you when you don't feel lovely. He loves you when no one else loves you. Others may abandon you, divorce you, and ignore you. But God will love you. Always. No matter what.

Max Lucado

It wasn't so long ago that I had to go around to the back door of a restaurant to order a hamburger just because my skin wasn't white. And there I stood, next to the garbage dumpster in the alley, waiting for my order.

As an ambitious young woman just out of high school and attempting to register at a secretarial school, I was so excited! I dressed up in my pretty blue dress and topped it all with my blue high-heeled shoes and pretty blue bag, confident that I could make a good impression and attend that school. But within minutes my young heart was crushed. Because of the color of my skin, I was unceremoniously escorted out of the office before I could even register.

It would have been easy to let one hurt pile upon another, and I have only shared two brief experiences of prejudice here. Imagine what the average Black person my age has endured. Contemplate the assault to their very personhood—and all based on the pigment of their skin.

It was tempting to flash my own weapons of anger and fight evil with evil, but as a Christian I read that the apostle Paul explained, "God is pleased when, conscious of His will, you patiently endure unjust treatment. Of course, you get no credit for being patient if you are beaten for doing wrong. But if you suffer for doing good and endure it patiently, God is pleased with you" (1 Peter 2:19–20 NLT).

The times I had to drink out of a water fountain labeled "Colored" because I might contaminate the water for white folks was just this kind of outrageous injustice. Did God want me and other Black folks just to take it? Dr. Martin Luther King Jr. didn't think so. I don't think so. But one thing I have learned through the years: We are free to hate. But as Christians isn't it more fitting to use our freedom to love?

Love is patient, love is kind. … It does not dishonor others, it is not self-seeking, it is not easily angered, it keeps no record of wrongs. Love does not delight in evil but rejoices with the truth. It always protects, always trusts, always hopes, always perseveres. Love never fails.

I CORINTHIANS 13:4–8

An Empowering Choice

– Cathy Gallagher –

*Cold words freeze people and hot words scorch them,
and bitter words make them bitter, and wrathful
words make them wrathful. ... Kind words also
produce their own image on men's souls.
And a beautiful image it is.*

Blaise Pascal

When I answered the phone, I recognized his voice and thought I was prepared for anything. I was wrong. After hearing his request, I was tempted to say mean words to my former employer and then slam down the receiver. I thought: *You've got to be kidding! Why would I do this for you after what you did to me? The nerve!*

My mind flashed back to three weeks earlier when the same company president who was on the phone called me into his office and said, "Cathy, six weeks ago I hired you as customer service director. You get here early. You stay late. You're always upbeat and you have a positive attitude. You've done some good things while you've been here, but you don't fit my culture. I'm letting you go."

I don't fit your culture? Why not? What does that mean? It didn't make sense. When he hired me, the president had said, "Cathy, you have all the skills and experience I had hoped to find in someone; you are *exactly* the person I am looking for." A few weeks later, he fired me.

Now, on the phone, the company president was making a bold, nervy request. "Cathy, you are a good writer, and your articles have been published. Will you write the story of my company and get it published in the industry journal I most want it to be in?"

My thoughts swirled. This was absurd. *You don't think I fit your culture, so you fired me. Now you want me to write for you? In your dreams! Why should I?*

I felt the same surge of hurtful anger on the phone I had felt while I was being fired. I also felt the same urge to say unkind words. When the man was firing me, however, I had forced myself to zip my lips and turn a favorite Bible verse into a silent prayer before I spoke. The prayer helped me get through that awful meeting with professional dignity.

On the phone now, I zipped my lips and prayed that same silent prayer I had prayed three weeks earlier: "May the words of my mouth and the meditation of my heart be pleasing to you, O Lord, my rock and my redeemer" (Psalm 19:14 NLT). Then I took a breath and quietly said, "Yes. I'll write your story and get it published." I had no idea what would happen next.

Usually the publishing process takes many months, but

not this time. I knew the journal and the types of stories the editor preferred. Several years earlier, at the editor's request, I had ghostwritten a story for this journal, so I felt comfortable presenting the story idea over the phone. The editor replied that she wanted this story if I could get it to her within a month. I assured her I could meet this deadline.

Writing the story involved interviewing the man who had fired me. As the twenty-seven-year-old president related the details of how he developed his business from a seed of an idea into a thriving six-million-dollar business in only eight years, I developed a new respect for him. I put aside my anger at being fired and focused on writing a story that would make us proud we had worked together.

Much to my delight and surprise, the editor gave the story the most prestigious spot in the tabloid-size journal—the center two-page spread. And she agreed to purchase a second story from me, which ended up getting published six months later.

The best part of this experience took place on the day I presented an advance copy of the journal to the company president. After he read the story, I asked if he liked it. His eyes danced when he said, "Oh, yes, Cathy. It is much more than I expected or ever dreamed possible."

It was more than I had expected too. The money the president paid me for writing his story, after I tithed my church, covered an entire month of living expenses, which was important since I was unemployed.

When I think about the choice I made to pray that my words would be pleasing, both on the day the company president fired me and again three weeks later when he made his request on the phone, I understand the relationship between my words and my life experiences. The words I choose either limit or expand my world. Mean words limit, but kind words can expand my horizons by opening doors of opportunity.

Be gracious in your speech. The goal is to bring out the best in others in a conversation, not put them down, not cut them out.

COLOSSIANS 4:6 MSG

Six Feet Tall—and Bald!

— Eva Marie Everson —

*Laughter is the shortest
distance between two people.*

Victor Borge

"Would you like to meet for lunch?" my friend Deb asked. "I'm going to be in your part of the world on Thursday, and I thought it'd be nice to get together."

Although Deb and I lived in the same city, there was a forty-five-minute distance between us. It seemed we were always looking for excuses to "get together."

"I'd love to," I answered.

"But let me warn you, it's too hot to wear a wig. I hope you don't mind being seen with a bald woman." My valiant friend had been successfully battling cancer. Chemo's only visible side effect? The loss of a full head of hair.

"I don't mind," I assured her.

A few days later I sat across the table from Deb in a booth at a local restaurant where we exchanged news about our families, our work, and ourselves. As overhead light cast reflections and halos about her head, she sat straight and tall, completely unfettered by the questioning stares of other patrons.

"I am determined to get through this with grace and humor," Deb told me. "So far ... so good."

"Excuse me," our waitress interrupted, looking at Deb. "Do you mind if I ask—do you have cancer? Are you undergoing chemo?"

"Yes, I am," Deb answered.

"Would you mind going to the hair salon? It's just a few shops away in this mall."

Our brows shot straight up. *Do what?*

"My friend—the owner—was just diagnosed with cancer ... and she's just not handling it well."

Deb smiled. "I'd be happy to!"

"I know you don't even know her," the waitress added.

"I always say there are no strangers in the world," Deb countered. "Just new friends I've yet to meet. Don't worry. Leave everything to me."

An hour later, I followed along as Deb, nearly six feet tall and completely bald, walked into the salon. "I'm here for a perm," she exclaimed to the gawking faces. Then she laughed. "I'd like to speak to the owner, please."

A petite, dark-haired woman approached us. "I am the owner," she said. "May I help you?"

Deb asked if there was a space where they could talk. "Someplace private?"

I could sense the woman was nervous. Why would a

bald woman want to talk to the owner of a hair salon? To buy a wig, perhaps? Hopefully not to complain about a hair product gone bad.

"Sure," she said. The woman escorted us to the back of the salon, where a small desk sat flanked by a few chairs among stacks of papers and boxes of shampoo and conditioner. "Will this do?"

Deb and I sat, and Deb got right to the point. "Your friend from Gleason's Restaurant asked me to come down and speak with you. I have cancer."

The shop owner, whose name tag read *Maria*, sat down. "I was just diagnosed," she said.

"I know." Deb's voice was steady. "I want to talk with you about that."

For the next half hour, Deb shared her story and then answered Maria's questions. Shoulders—straight with tension when we'd first sat down—inched downward. In no time Maria was laughing at Deb's anecdotes and sharing some of her own more humorous moments of dealing with the disease they shared. Finally, Deb asked, "Can we pray with you?"

Maria nodded. "Please."

We prayed together before being escorted from the back of the shop, past the boxes of stored product and down a wide aisle between sinks and salon chairs. All eyes were on us, appearing to hold a question. *What was so funny back there?*

Just as we reached the front door, it swung open, and a distinguished gentleman walked in. He took one look at Deb and stopped short.

"I'd run the other way if I were you," Deb said, loud enough for everyone to hear. "When I came in, I had long hair. All I asked for was a trim!" She ran her hand over her smooth, shining head.

The man only gawked.

Deb never blinked nor missed a beat. "Seriously!"

"Hey!" Maria called from behind us, laughing. "You'll run off all my customers."

Over her shoulder Deb returned a smile, then cut her eyes back to the man. "I'm just kidding," she said with a chuckle. "I just have cancer."

When we turn our trials over to God, He truly *does* turn our heartache into laughter, even if it means sending a bald woman into a hair-styling salon.

> *God has brought me laughter, and everyone who hears about this will laugh with me.*
>
> GENESIS 21:6

Changing Lives Without Leaving Home

— Maggie Wallem Rowe —

The devil is outrageous only against prayer, and those that exercise it; because he knows it is the true means of taking his prey from him.

Madame Jeanne Guyon

Whenever the phone rang on Friday afternoons promptly at 4:00 p.m., I always knew who was on the other end, though I often had to strain to hear her.

"Hello, dearie!" came the soft voice, pausing to pull air into her lungs. "I know you're busy, but how are all the children? And you and Pastor? How may I pray for you this week?"

Now well into her eighties, the caller was simply known as Grandma Sue. Other than Pat, her loving daughter-in-law with whom she lived, Sue had no blood relatives in our 150-year-old church on Cape Cod. Congestive heart failure and failing eyesight prevented her from attending weekly services, yet practically everyone in the congregation knew

Sue. Or knew *of* her. Her fervent ministry of intercessory prayer kept her connected to the life of our active church.

At the time, my husband and I had five teenagers at home. Monitoring their many needs and myriad activities along with caring for our church family left us exhausted. Whenever Sue called, I'd slump in relief against the kitchen wall, treasuring the conversation I knew would end too soon.

Always sensitive to the frenzied pace of our lives, Sue brushed off inquiries about her own health so she could focus on our family's needs. Since her eyesight was degenerating, Sue didn't write down prayer concerns but rather committed them to memory. Each Friday she would follow up on the items I'd mentioned during our previous conversation, never forgetting a single detail. Each call ended the same way, with Sue exclaiming, "Oodles of love!"

To a pastor's family that couldn't keep up with the many demands upon our lives, those regular prayer calls were a lifeline. We were stretched in every conceivable direction, but Sue's faithful prayers lifted us up to the one place we most needed to be—the throne of God.

"How fortunate we are to have someone in our church family like Sue!" I would comment to my husband. "How many pastors have a member who dedicates themselves to praying for their family?"

But the day came when Sue's weakened heart no longer could support her unflagging spirit. Just as we had often visited Sue at her home, we kept vigil with Pat at Cape Cod Hospital while Sue's breathing grew increasingly labored. Nearly blind now, Sue could not focus on our presence. But it was obvious she continued to keep company with the God who had been her lifelong companion.

When the call came that Grandma Sue had gone to be with the One whom she loved and served, our teenage children cried with us.

"Can we skip school and come to her funeral?" one asked. "She hadn't been to church in so long. There might not be many people at her service who really knew her anymore. We want to be there for her."

Permission was granted. Our family of seven filled an entire pew in remembrance of the woman who had been an honorary grandmother and, even more importantly, our personal prayer warrior.

We were surprised, then, to watch as the sanctuary began to fill—and then swell to several hundred in attendance. Following Sue's favorite hymns, my husband shared the gospel message, just as she had requested. He lifted the microphone from its stand and invited anyone who wanted to share a memory of Sue to come forward.

The steady stream of people resembled an altar call. One after the other, church members, neighbors, and friends stepped up to the mic to pay tribute to the woman they, too, called Grandma Sue.

"She prayed for me every Monday."

"I always looked forward to Thursdays, when Sue called to ask how she could pray for us."

"Saturdays were when we always talked to Sue. She was like our prayer grandmother!"

Astonished, members of the congregation gazed at one another. Unbeknownst to any of us, the little lady shut in at home with macular degeneration and congestive heart failure had the most far-reaching ministry of anyone in our church. Each of us thought we were the only ones Sue prayed for. Truth be told, there must have been *hundreds* on her list.

Only God knows how many lives were changed because of the persistent intercession of one faithful, loving woman. The telephone was her ministry. Prayer was her superpower.

And all of Sue's calls concluded in the very same way: "Oodles of love!"

The prayer of a righteous person
is powerful and effective.

JAMES 5:16

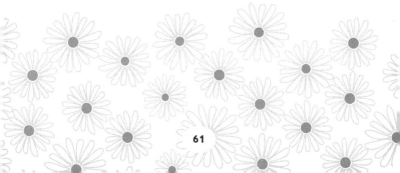

Defiant Ways

– Melissa Sutter Brower –

"Parents who are afraid to put their foot down usually have children who step on toes."

A Chinese proverb

Mom slipped into the seat behind the wheel of our old Chevy Impala and suddenly remembered something important. "Kids, I left my purse in the house. I'll be right back." My brother Danny and I were already in the backseat.

The two minutes it was going to take for her to run in and get her purse was more than enough time for me, a "sweet" six-year-old girl, to develop a master plan and obtain the cooperation of my five-year-old brother.

As Mom entered the house and shut the door, I looked directly at my brother and said, with a quite serious tone, "I feel like swearing."

Since my parents did not swear, our swearing vocabulary was limited. However, like my mom always said, "If you set your mind to doing something, you can do it!" I started the naughty banter by calling my brother a couple of words I was confident my parents would have cringed at and called "cuss words." That was all it took. Danny joined right in my fun little name-calling game by returning a sentence with his own nasty little words. Back and forth the swearing went as we laughed and laughed.

Suddenly, between giggles, we heard a familiar but sickening sound. It was the "Uh-hum" sound only an angry mother can make. Yes, our mom was standing outside the car, and unfortunately, the car window was down! She had been listening to our new little game and did not think it was nearly as funny as we had only a few seconds earlier.

How she managed to open a car door, grab both of us by the arms, and haul us through the house at such great speed, I will never know! It felt as though my feet were flapping behind me as my long hair blew in the wind. Instantly we were transported to the bathroom. I had no idea what the consequences would be for our misbehavior, but I was confident I wouldn't like it. Eyes open wide, lips sucked in, and hands covering our behinds, we waited for our sentencing.

Mom very calmly told us that swearing was not allowed and that we would learn what soap tasted like as a reminder to keep our language clean. Being a strong-willed child, I thought this sounded more like a *challenge* than a *punishment*.

Holding the bar of soap up to Danny, Mom didn't have to say anything. In compliance, he licked the soap, made a wrinkly-nosed face, and sweetly apologized to Mom.

It was my turn. Not wanting her to think I was distressed

with the punishment, I smiled as Mom held up the soap. Instead of licking it, I determined the best way to make my point was by biting off an entire corner of the bar—which I did with great determination and vigor. Familiar with my defiant ways, Mom let me chew. And chew. And chew. The soap did not taste good. As a matter of fact, it was intolerable. Mom noticed the color leaving my cheeks and knew I was about to lose my breakfast.

"Spit it out," she demanded.

Between gags I choked out, "No! I like it!"

"Spit it out, Melissa Sue!" she pleaded, more urgently this time.

"No, it's good," I insisted, as the multiplying suds began to escape my mouth.

"Melissa!" Her request came too late. I suppressed a final gag and then proceeded to redecorate our bathroom.

I'm not sure which of us learned the greater lesson. I quit swearing. My mom never made me eat soap again. Of course, I was only six, and I still had many more lessons to learn.

Thinking back over my behavior in front of Danny that day, I wonder, how many times have I set a poor example? How often have I been gagging on something nasty in my life, insisting I like it? How many times has God tried to correct me, teach me, or lead me, only to have me spit the lesson out because of my stubborn ways?

For people who hate discipline
and only get more stubborn,
There'll come a day when life
tumbles in and they break, but by
then it'll be too late to help them.

PROVERBS 29:1 MSG

My Front Porch Family

— Thelma Wells —

*There it was: the faith, the encouragement, these strands of
reassurance woven into a network of mutual support.
Nobody had to face anything without allies whose
loyalty was beyond question. Nobody was ever alone.*

Arthur Gordon

Though I wouldn't wish the days of segregation on anyone, perhaps the one blessing in this period of history was that in small Black communities, we looked out for each other with an urgent watchfulness. In my neighborhood, if you didn't know what you were doing, honey, you can be sure somebody else did.

I'll never forget the day I was about nine years old and walking down the street in my pretty ruffled dress, feeling as safe as a little chick in a coop of friendly folks who cared about me. Then a sleek, black Cadillac, with longhorns on its hood, pulled up slowly alongside me. The driver leaned across the seat to roll down the window and offer me a ride. I glanced at him, curious, but kept walking. At this point, he stopped the car and said, "Hey, little girl, come here."

Shrugging, I took a step toward the car and leaned on the door to look inside. But before I could say a word, I heard a shriek that rattled the street.

Althea Hilliard, a friend of my family, had observed the scene from the dental office where she worked as a hygienist and rushed out the door. She now hurtled herself toward me like a wild, mad hen on a mission.

"You get yourself away from here, girl!" Frantically, she waved her arms in my direction, shooing off invading forces of evil in our midst. When Althea finally reached me, she took hold of my arms, squeezing them in a vice-like grip until we were eyeball to eyeball, nose to nose. "And don't you ever let me see you hangin' on this car or talkin' to this man again, you hear? Not this man or any other man, understand?"

All I could manage, with fear rising in my eyes and pain throbbing in my arms, was a tremulous, "Yes, ma'am."

Then Althea turned to the man in the car and let loose on him the way only a furious hen—or an angry Black mama—can. If Althea had not been watching out for me, who knows what might have happened to me and my girl-hood innocence that afternoon?

The men of our neighborhood were equally protective. If I dawdled on the way home and passed Mr. Bodden's shoe shop later than usual, Mr. Bodden greeted me with a frown and a scolding. "School's been out for a half an hour, little girl," he'd say, nodding toward the clock on his shop wall. "You go on, now. I'm going to stand here and watch till you get home."

The eyes of my neighborhood were ever upon me—watching, observing, caring.

I don't think I grasped the value of this until I was an adult and realized my life had been lived in front of a community that valued its children. I can't help but wonder what a difference it would make if every young person today could know they have "Someone to Watch Over Me." And not just *one* someone, but a *bunch* of someones.

For, indeed, it takes a front-porch village of mamas, daddies, aunts, uncles, ministers, teachers, shop owners, and, yes, dental hygienists to raise children in the way they should go.

My eyes will watch over them for their good.

JEREMIAH 24:6

Go, Granny, Go!

– Gracie Malone –

If only we could go back to the time when mistakes could be corrected by simply exclaiming, "Do over!"

Unknown

I'd picked up my five-year-old grandson, Luke, after school, buckled him snugly in the back of my car, and was heading home when I rounded a curve a bit too fast. When my car swerved, he slapped his hand on his forehead and groaned, "Grandma Gracie, slow down. Don't you know curves are dangerous?" Before I could even apologize, he added, "I'd hate for anything to happen to you."

Of course, Luke was right! I made a vow right then and there never to speed when one of my grandchildren occupied the backseat. Unfortunately, when I'm alone my mind sometimes drifts into a daydream, old habits take over, and I get going a bit too fast.

It was after such an occasion recently that I called our son Jason—the one I can usually count on to be sensitive and understanding. "Son," I began sweetly, "could you explain what 'deferred adjudication' means?"

Instead of giving me a straightforward answer, my bright young college student burst out laughing and asked, "How many speeding tickets have you gotten, Mom?"

"Just two," I whined, "but they were biggies—one in a school zone, of all things, and the other, well ... in a construction zone."

"Mom, what were you thinking?"

"Sometimes my mind wanders! Anyway, I've already taken care of the school zone offense by taking a defensive driving class online. But now ... well ..." I took a deep breath and continued. "I was running late for a hair appointment and didn't even notice the guys placing orange cones on the road—until, that is, I saw a motorcycle cop do a U-ey and flash his red and blue lights. As I pulled onto the shoulder, I couldn't help but notice the officer's fine leather jacket and black, shiny boots, so I ran my fingers through my hair, pasted on my best smile, and lowered the window to say good morning."

"Mom, you didn't try to charm him out of a ticket, did you?" Jason asked.

"Well. Not exactly ..."

For the next few minutes, I gave just enough detail to incur Jason's sympathy and obtain the information I needed. After I hung up, my mind returned to the scene of the crime. I had not tried to charm the officer. But while I was fumbling for my driver's license, I *had* decided to get something off my chest.

"Sir," I began to say in a matter-of-fact tone, "may I say just one thing?"

"Sure, ma'am."

"Well ..." I smoothed the wrinkles in my skirt and sucked in a huge gulp of air. "The cars in front of me were driving the same speed I was."

The officer shook his head and grinned. "I know that, lady, but I can only catch you people one at a time." He handed over the citation, turned on his well-polished heels, and remounted his bike.

I slipped my car in gear and proceeded—very slowly—down the road toward the beauty shop. A few days later I appeared in court, ready to ask for deferred adjudication.

The judge peered over her glasses as she addressed our group of malefactors seated in the courtroom—who, I might add, were mostly *young* and *male*. "Don't even think about not telling the truth," she began, "because we have records of every offense you've committed in the state of Texas." She cleared her throat and added, "Speak up when you address the court."

My heart pounded as I waited my turn.

When the bailiff finally called my name, I stepped to the bench. Speaking fast and a bit too loud, I rattled off the four driving violations—only four, mind you—of my entire life, including one for an out-of-date inspection sticker.

The judge was not impressed with my record or with my honesty. "Probation for one hundred twenty days!" she declared. Then she pointed her bony finger at me and added, "We'll be watching you!"

As I paid my fine and headed out the door, I felt like a real criminal. Throughout the next four months I had to deal with my misgivings: How could I, a protective mother and doting grandmother who preached caution to her offspring, end up a reckless speed demon on wheels? I also endured unmerciful teasing from the men in our family. It began as soon as I got home from court when I called Jason and asked, "Now, what does probation mean?"

Be a good citizen. All governments are under God.
Insofar as there is peace and order, it's God's order. So live
responsibly as a citizen.... Duly constituted authorities are
only a threat if you're trying to get by with something.
Decent citizens should have nothing to fear.

ROMANS 13:1–3 MSG

Battle of the Ding Dongs

– Rachel St. John-Gilbert –

If you lose the power to laugh, you lose the power to think.

Clarence Darrow

An author friend graciously offered to review my manuscript for a book of humorous devotionals. Well-versed in English and grammar, she was stumped by the term *Ding Dong*, referring to one of the cream-filled chocolate cakes made by Hostess, which I had chosen to hyphenate. Not finding it in her volume of *Hyphenated Words for the Hyperactive Hyphenator,* Lynn had a stroke of genius.

She called her husband, who was on his way to the grocery store. Newly health-conscious, Mike was on a mission in search of low-fat foods to prolong not only his life but that of his wife and their young daughter, Sheridan.

Phone in hand, Lynn was on the case. "Michael, dear, I'm so glad you've arrived at the store. I'm working on Rachel's book and need to know if *Ding Dongs* are hyphenated."

Multitasking Michael, who was now browsing the rice cake aisle with cell phone in hand, didn't hesitate. "Lynn, of course Ding Dongs are hydrogenated—but it doesn't matter. I'm not buying any—Sheridan doesn't need to be eating that junk anyway."

Lynn and I had a good laugh—but the story doesn't stop there. We each began to sense the seed of a good story germinating. But *whose* story was it?

You've got to understand. I was raised in a family of wordsmith vultures, always circling the dinner table, coffee table, Ping-Pong table (you name it) looking for fodder for a chapter, an essay, or a blockbuster title. Whenever someone uttered funny or insightful material, we would scramble like puppies chasing the chuckwagon in search of a napkin and pen to jot down the literary morsel. If we couldn't find paper, we would write on our hands because the unwritten rule of thumb (so to speak) was that whoever wrote it down first got to use the goods.

Believe me, it could get pretty crazy with several writers in the hunt. We even developed our own version of Miranda rights to read to our friends and relatives. Upon whipping out our pens to record that catchy phrase, wrap up that witticism, or capture the coveted laugh-out-loud funny, we warned: "Any slightly humorous, entertaining, or profound utterance from your mouth can and will be considered fair game for publication in one of our stories. But we promise not to use it against you!"

So, back to poor Lynn. She, too, is a writing scavenger who can spot publishable prey a mile away, and, after all, it was *her* husband who unwittingly coughed up the cutie. Yet

I really wanted to use the *hydrogenated* slipup in my own book. What to do with our ding-dong dilemma? Well, in the spirit of friendship, Lynn decided not to prolong the battle of the Ding Dongs. Instead, she consented to let me use the incident here and now, as a gift to you—but only after I signed over the rights to my firstborn grandchild. Sheeze! It's brutal out there in Christian publishing.

And is *Ding Dong* hyphenated? As you see in this story, sometimes yes, sometimes no. Just don't ask me to explain when! Go ask your grammar teacher.

Would that we pursued the things of God with the same single-minded focus of writers desperate for good material. Would that we treasured Scripture, reveled in the power of prayer, and immersed ourselves in the joy of sharing Christ's love with others. Perhaps we should write our own Miranda rights: Anything *God* says can and will be used to make me all that I was created to be—to the glory of God and the blessing of those around me.

> It's in Christ that we find out who we
> are and what we are living for.
>
> EPHESIANS 1:11 MSG

Mom's Medal

– Carol Kent –

Making the decision to have a child—it's momentous.
It is to decide forever to have your heart
go walking around outside your body.

Elizabeth Stone

I liked Donna immediately. Her sense of humor was so contagious that anyone within six feet of her was caught up in the fun of whatever was happening at that moment.

A single mom, Donna worked in the book department of an international ministry. We were both mothers of sons, and it didn't take long before we shared our anxieties about seeing our sons grow up and face difficult decisions in a fast-changing world.

Donna told me about her fears when her son, Barrett, joined the US Air Force and was sent to boot camp in San Antonio, Texas. He was the squad leader for the barracks and often told his mom, "These guys don't know how to make a bed, polish their boots or their brass, or do pretty much any routine household task. Almost everybody in my squad owes me a pizza for helping them pass inspection!"

Barrett only met one other Christian during the six weeks he was in boot camp. The Saturday night before graduation he called to let his mom know his flight was going to have their first leave.

That night Donna called to tell her mother the news. Her mom put words to Donna's fears. "Well, honey, you know what those young servicemen are like. They've been cooped up for several weeks and now they have an off-base pass. They will be going to town to drink, and they'll be looking for women. You know they will be 'whooping it up,' and they'll want Barrett to go with them, and they'll try to get him to drink."

Donna tried to calm her mom while subduing her own anxious heart. "Mom, you know that Barrett is grounded in God's Word. Don't worry, we know he would never get into that kind of trouble." After saying goodbye, she sighed, "Oh, dear!" and prayed for her young son.

On the first night of Barrett's leave from boot camp, Donna's phone rang. When she answered, her son's voice boomed on the other end of the line. "Hi, Mom!" he said cheerfully. "Well, we're finally having our first leave!" Her heart fluttered at the sound of loud laughter and commotion in the background.

He went on. "Most of the guys went into town, but my friend and I decided to stay in the barracks to polish our brass. We're trying hard to make 'honor graduate'!"

Donna's heart returned to a normal rate of speed as she

was reminded of all the prayers she'd sent up for her boy. God was answering ... and He would continue to answer.

Three years after joining the Air Force, Sergeant William Barrett Goddard sent his mother the following letter:

Dear Mom,

Before you read on, open the package: This is something I want you to have. It's my first medal, and I would really like you to have it. It's called the Air Force Good Conduct Medal. It was granted to me for three years of perfect service to the Air Force. When I say "perfect," I mean three years without a blemish on my record. In other words, I conducted myself in the proper Air Force manner for three consecutive years.

I want you to have this for a couple of reasons. First, you've supported me more than anyone ... in my Air Force career. You've always accepted what I had to do, and I felt it was most appropriate to tell you what my plans were first.

The second reason is simple. You raised me in such a manner that I didn't have to do anything to earn this medal other than to be myself. ... You earned this medal as much as I did. So please accept it.

Love,

Barrett

Barrett eventually became a coach, a husband, and a father of three. His oldest son, Nathan, graduated from kindergarten *with honors.*

Point your kids in the right direction—
When they're old they won't be lost.

PROVERBS 22:6 MSG

Morning Smiles

– Pauline Afman –

You can't deny laughter; when it comes, it plops down in your favorite chair and stays as long as it wants.

Stephen King

It was a lazy morning, and I stayed in bed long after I awoke, enjoying the cool air coming in my bedroom window. The doorbell rang. I heard my husband open the front door. Evidently, a county work crew was trimming tree limbs along the road to ward off problems with electrical lines. They requested permission to cut some branches from the maple tree standing majestically on our front lawn.

Since I couldn't quite hear what was being said and was feeling a bit nosy, I threw on my robe and peeked into the living room. Arriving just as the door closed, I thought, *I got out of my warm bed for* this?

When my husband left to make his rounds at the hospital and the nursing home as visitation pastor, I decided to get comfortable in my living room lounge chair. Before long I snuggled under a soft, cozy blanket and fell fast asleep.

The doorbell startled me out of a sound sleep. Glancing

at the clock, I was amazed to discover an hour and a half had gone by since I sat down in my recliner. I wasn't even dressed! But someone was definitely at the door, and they weren't leaving.

Oh, well. My robe was more like a housedress and completely covered me, so I opened the door. There stood a handsome young man, one of the workers on the tree-trimming crew. He just wanted to verify that it was all right to cut off some maple limbs. I assured him it was fine. The young man had the oddest look on his face—quizzical? No, more like *amused*!

I hurried to the bathroom and looked in the mirror. My scant hair was standing straight up. I looked like a grandma sporting a very unattractive spike! What would my style-conscious grandsons think if they saw me now? I grinned at myself, thinking I now knew why that young man was chuckling.

A moment later, however, I discovered the *real* reason for his amusement. I had forgotten to put in my false teeth. Horrors! With my gums grinning back at me, I thought, *Appearance might not be everything, but in this case, it's quite a bit!* I blushed like a young girl and laughed out loud.

Fortunately, at my advanced age there aren't many people I still feel the need to impress. I know outward beauty is fleeting, but I think I'll make it a priority to look in the mirror *before* I answer the door anytime soon. After all, it might be one of my cute grandsons!

*What matters is not your outer appearance—the styling
of your hair, the jewelry you wear, the cut of your clothes—
but your inner disposition. Cultivate inner beauty,
the gentle, gracious kind that God delights in.*

I PETER 3:3–4 MSG

The Birdcage Christmas Tree

— Ginger Shaw —

Attitudes are the quiet judgments that shape our lives;
they mold the form that living takes.

Found in a church bulletin

I stood there staring. What was that thing hanging from the stairs above the atrium? Black wrought iron covered with a gold garland, shiny colored ornaments hanging around its edges, and filled with small, wrapped packages. I looked at my sister. She rolled her eyes and shrugged. I looked at my mother. Her eyes shone brightly as she said, "It's a Christmas tree!"

Oh, yeah. Right. A Christmas tree?

Well, it *was* Christmas Eve. We had just returned from a midnight church service. But it didn't feel like Christmas. And this certainly didn't look like a tree. Two feet high? Black metal? What a pathetic tree!

Our holidays had always been different by most standards. We moved so often we seldom knew where we would be or what to expect. But we always had our immediate family—my dad, mother, two sisters, and me. And we always had a fresh, green Christmas tree. Our small family holidays were precious times to each of us.

But this year we had just arrived in Bangkok, Thailand—not exactly your winter wonderland. My dad was on a mission with the Air Force, flying out of Laos and unable to come home for the holidays. My older sister was in college in the States. What little extended family we had was scattered across the US. Even our dog was lost in transit and wouldn't arrive for several days. So there we stood—my mother, my younger sister, and me. Alone. Christmas Eve. In a Buddhist country on the far side of the world. No friends. No dog. No Christmas fun. What a pathetic holiday!

My gaze returned to the "tree." I wondered what my mother was thinking. Had the heat gotten to her? Had she contracted some exotic disease? Had she gone crazy?

She tried to explain. "Evergreen trees don't grow on this tropical land. They're not imported because Buddhists have no need of Christmas trees." She told us the artificial trees, received at the military commissary in July, had been purchased quickly by the savvy families who probably endured a treeless Christmas the year before.

So my resourceful mother decided to create her own version of a Christmas tree. Mother has always loved wrought iron, and in Bangkok you could have it made to order. I thought perhaps this was just an excuse to add more of it to her collection. But she insisted it was her Christmas spirit that prompted her to design this birdcage to hang beneath the stairs in our temporary home. She dug through the unpacked boxes to find our decorations and hung the newly wrought birdcage above the indoor atrium. Finally, she filled the inside with small, brightly wrapped boxes. Notice I said *boxes*, not gifts. The one moment of excitement at the sight of all the presents faded quickly as Mother told us they were just for decoration.

What a pathetic holiday!

This was the first Christmas our family wasn't all together. I'd like to say we were like the family in *Little Women*, thankful and joyful for our little birdcage Christmas tree, gathered around the atrium singing carols—but memory tells me otherwise.

Looking back, I know it wasn't an easy holiday for my mother, and I know my attitude didn't make it any easier. But her determination to make the best of all circumstances, wherever and with whatever God provided, profoundly impacts my life—even to this day. And it made her a *great* military wife. I've seen it through countless changes—moves, illness, and widowhood.

I don't remember many of the presents I've received over the years, but I do remember the gift of the birdcage Christmas tree. And today it hangs in my office to remind me not of that pitiful holiday but of the priceless gift Mother passed on to me—a positive attitude!

*Be cheerful no matter what; pray all the time;
thank God no matter what happens. This is the way
God wants you who belong to Christ Jesus to live.*

I THESSALONIANS 5:16–18 MSG

In-Flight Friendship

— Charlotte Adelsperger —

*Be kind. Remember everyone you
meet is fighting a hard battle.*

Ian MacLaren

When our plane took off from Kansas City for Newark, New Jersey, my heart pounded with excitement. *Tomorrow—Germany!* My husband, Bob, squeezed my hand. I ignored the young woman seated next to me who wore sunglasses and obviously wanted to be left alone.

After the usual airline snack, I flipped open a notebook full of German phrases.

"Looks like you're studying German," my seatmate said, peering over darkened lenses.

"Right." I told her about our trip and how I was brushing up for my visit with a friend who lived near Frankfurt.

"I studied in Frankfurt for three years," she said enthusiastically. She told me she was from Kenya and was on her way home.

"Could you help me with my German?" I asked.

She did just that, and she was a natural! We both

launched into guttural sounds, smiles, and chuckles.

The humor of it all struck me. *Here I am flying across the country, learning German words from a young woman from Africa!*

I asked her name. "Caroline," she said, then her voice turned serious. "You've helped me more than you know. You see, when I got on the plane, I couldn't stop crying. You got my mind on other things." She explained how hard it was to leave both her brother and her sister who remained in the United States.

Caroline asked me about values in American culture, and I discovered we were both Christians. I could tell she was well educated with strong faith in God. On the lighter side, we discovered we both love to play tennis. Caroline was young enough to be my daughter, but we seemed to connect on every topic.

While our plane descended, Caroline pulled out a business card. She explained that it was from an American gentleman who had visited Kenya. "Do you know anything about this group?" she asked, pointing to the logo.

"That's a Christian organization I know well! I write for its magazines. This is amazing!" Quickly we shared our experiences.

Soon our plane landed in Newark. While we waited for our connecting flights, Bob and I enjoyed our time with Caroline and treated her to her first root beer float.

"This is so good!" she said between sips. "Why didn't

my brother or sister ever tell me about these?" Despite her chuckle, her eyes still glimmered with a shadow of sadness.

When she and I stopped in the ladies' restroom, no one else was there. I noticed Caroline washing her hands at the far end of the long rectangular room.

All of a sudden, a playful spirit swept over me, and in pantomime I "hit" a tennis ball the length of the room to her. She pivoted to the right position, extended her arm, and returned the imaginary shot. We broke into laughter. Back and forth we swung our invisible rackets. As I jumped for a high shot, a woman walked in. She froze, speechless.

What a sight—two women from different generations, races, and nationalities swinging at each other and jumping around on the tile floor of a public restroom!

Before going to our separate gates, Caroline and I exchanged addresses. I hated to leave her—my delightful new friend. We hugged and promised to pray for each other.

When we returned from Europe, Caroline emailed: "I'm really excited that you have written to me. I thank the Lord for putting you in my path. You encourage me so much and you make me actually believe that life is all about people. You made my flight from America all the more bearable."

I was touched by her words and felt privileged to know her. We wrote often and shared prayer requests and dreams.

To my surprise, a year later Caroline flew to America with her father, Joseph, to attend her sister's college graduation. During the Christmas holidays, all three of them were able to see us in Kansas City. At our home we savored our time together and sipped tea from Kenya. Later we ate dinner and took in the Christmas lights. My heart sang when I discovered more about our guests' close walk with the Lord.

After the holidays Caroline wrote, "You both are really like part of my family now. You have become more special to me as the days have gone by." That spirit continues in both of us.

I often think back to that joyful evening with Caroline and her family. At the end of our time together, she asked us to join in prayer. Words flowed in thanksgiving to God, and in my spirit, I was again lifted in flight.

If I ride the wings of the morning,
if I dwell by the farthest oceans,
even there your hand will guide me,
and your strength will support me.

PSALM 139:9–10 NLT

90

The New Neighbor

– Judy Hampton –

A good friend is my nearest relation.

Thomas Fuller

Hearing the sound of air brakes hissing outside my kitchen window, I glanced outside. A huge moving van had parked across our street.

Great! New neighbors were finally moving into that empty house.

Before the movers could unlock the huge doors on the back of the truck, our children, Doug and Joani, walked right over to check out the situation.

They returned soon with good news. "Mom, they have kids the same age as Doug and me," Joani said. "I already like them!"

It wasn't long before I met their mom, a Swedish beauty with shimmering blonde hair, periwinkle eyes, and a welcoming smile. "Hi, there, I'm Judy Hampton," I said, greeting her warmly.

"My name is Judy too!" she exclaimed. In a matter of minutes, we discovered we had a lot in common. As the weeks passed, our kids played together endlessly. My new neighbor was either coming to my house to get her two children or I was walking across the street to retrieve mine. We always had time for a brief visit. Judy and I would pick up right where we left off the day before. She loved being a mom, wife, and homemaker, and I soon discovered Judy was the quintessential housekeeper.

In time our conversation turned to spiritual things. I was a fairly new Christian, passionate to share how Christ had changed my life. Judy listened attentively.

"We're a religious family too," she replied matter-of-factly. But from that point on, our conversations always moved to other issues.

Mondays always found me doing endless piles of laundry and cleaning my house. I loved getting household tasks done in one day so I could free up the rest of the week for more important things. On one Monday, I stood at my kitchen sink loading the dishwasher. Beyond the window, I noticed Judy placing something in the mailbox on my front porch. Quickly I ran to the front door. "Hi, there!" I said enthusiastically. "Do you have a surprise for me?"

"Well, not exactly," she said. "My father-in-law died recently, and my mother-in-law gave us his car. I was vacuuming the trunk when I came across this religious book. I thought you might like it because you are so religious."

I stood there dazed, trying to visualize someone actually vacuuming out the trunk of a car. I couldn't recall ever doing such a thing. "Thanks, Judy. That's so thoughtful of you." The book was one I had already read, but I didn't have the heart to tell her.

Thinking quickly, I added, "Judy, I just read a book *you* might enjoy. It's very practical and insightful. It's taught me so much about what God says about the family. Would you like to read it?"

"Thanks! I love to read," she responded enthusiastically.

After dashing to our bookcase and retrieving it for her, I waved goodbye and resumed my endless list of chores. About two hours later there was a knock at my door. I was a bit miffed at the interruption to my routine. I opened the door and there stood Judy, tears streaming down her face.

"Oh, my goodness, what's the matter?" I gasped.

"Nothing's wrong. I just started reading the book and found I couldn't put it down. I read straight through to the very last page. I realized today what was missing in my life—a relationship with Jesus Christ! The author offered a simple prayer to receive Him as Savior, and I prayed the prayer right in my living room. Judy, I can't describe how I feel, but I am so excited! I have been laughing and crying at the same time. I knew I had to tell you."

By now tears were streaming down my face too. No wonder they call it the "Good News!"

That day, God made us family. Judy was my new sister in Christ.

I find myself praying for you with a glad heart. ...
There has never been the slightest doubt in my
mind that the God who started this great
work in you would keep at it and bring it to a
flourishing finish on the very day Christ Jesus appears.

PHILIPPIANS 1:4, 6 MSG

The Mouth that Roared

– Carol Kent –

Did you know that your words are shaping other people's lives?
That they are the mirrors in which others see themselves?
Every day you can speak life into their souls or suck
the life right out of them. The choice is yours.

Sharon Jaynes

Mary waddled up to the front of the sanctuary after my Bible study lecture. I found myself wondering if she would be stopping by the hospital to deliver her baby on the way home from the church.

"Carol, do you have time to talk?" she asked.

"Sure, I'd love to. How are you feeling?"

"Pregnant—*very pregnant.*"

I knew this had been an unexpected and difficult pregnancy for her. She had two preschoolers at home already, and the prospect of a newborn on top of her current pressures seemed a bit overwhelming. We took seats on the front pew.

She blurted out, "Do you know what God's been teaching me through our Bible study this year?"

"What's that?" I was curious to know if anything I had been saying was making a difference in somebody's life.

"He's been telling me that I need to get rid of the Nah-Nahs."

"What did you say?" She was using a phrase that wasn't in my vocabulary, and I doubted it was in the dictionary.

"You know, I'm big and fat and pregnant and uncomfortable and grouchy, and I get up in the morning feeling so-o-o-o terrible, and I go 'Nah-Nah! When is this baby going to be born and give me back my former self? I go into my children's room and trip over their toys and messes and dirty clothes, and I go, 'Nah-Nah! This place looks like a pigsty. It's time to get up and clean up this room!'"

She continued. "I gripe through their breakfast and complain while I make their peanut butter and jelly sandwiches for lunch. I Nah-Nah when my back hurts, and I yell at those kids for being normal two- and three-year-olds. When John comes home, I put leftovers on the table.

"He says, 'Oh, leftovers *again*?'

"And I respond, 'Nah-Nah—if you don't like them, you can cook for yourself!'"

Her hands were folded over the top of her gigantic belly. I wondered how she could keep breathing so easily with such a bundle to carry around. There were tears in her eyes as her voice softened. "As I was doing my Bible study assignment this week, I realized that I am a *terrible* person to live with. I wake up in the morning Nah-Nah-ing to my kids, I go through my day Nah-Nah-ing while I make meals, clean up the house, do laundry, and when I greet my husband. *I don't even like living with myself anymore!*"

Mary didn't need counseling. She needed a listening ear. I nodded to indicate I certainly understood where she was coming from. "After I finished my Bible study," she went on, "I got down on my knees beside the bed—and I'm so pregnant I can hardly assume that position—and I lifted my open hands to the Lord and prayed, 'Lord, You take the Nah-Nahs. I do not want to be a woman with negative words on my tongue day and night. I don't want my children to leave home someday thinking how happy they are to get away from such a whining, complaining mother. I don't want my husband to dread coming home.

"I want to be a woman with praise and affirmation on her lips. It's my desire to have my children remember that I celebrated their accomplishments and applauded their efforts. Help me to be a mother who reflects joy, peace, and serenity—instead of disapproval, irritation, and criticism. Put a guard on my tongue. Fill my mouth with tributes to You and to those I love."

That day Mary understood a principle that takes some of us years to learn. Words can harm or words can heal. Words can tear down, or words can build up. The choice is ours.

Do not let any unwholesome talk come out of your mouths, but only what is helpful for building others up according to their needs, that it may benefit those who listen.

EPHESIANS 4:29

Come to Supper, Child

— Thelma Wells —

*Turn your eyes upon Jesus,
look full in His wonderful face.*

Helen H. Lemmel

"Humble" comes from the word *hummus*, meaning "earth" or "brought down low."

Yes, the Creator of the universe who flung the stars into space is also a very down-to-earth God. Why was Jesus "brought down low"—why did He come down to earth in our form?

I was pondering this thought one day as I was busy in the kitchen, my "hive of five" grandkids buzzing around the living room. I put dinner on the table and gave the "y'all come" signal. My grown children and their children began to make their way toward the feast and the smells of my home-cooked turnip greens, buttered carrots, okra gumbo, mashed potatoes, brisket, baked chicken, and corn bread (with ice cream waiting in the freezer to top it all off a little later!).

But two of my darlin's were too busy playing to answer

the call. "Alyssa! Alaya!" I called again. Still, they paid no attention. So I did the only thing I could do. I went over to where they were engrossed in their baby dolls and scooted down on my achy ol' knees to look them in the eyes.

Now I had their full attention. "Girls," I said with loving firmness, "did you not hear me calling you?"

They shook their heads no, their dark braids flying, their brown eyes wide with surprise.

"Well, sweet things, now that I have your attention, help your old Grammy up and let's go eat."

Together the girls tugged on my arms, and off we went toward the banquet.

As I walked with them, I thought about having to go to all that trouble to physically scoot down low to get the attention of my granddaughters. It was then I realized that this is exactly what Jesus did for me.

God had a wonderful feast prepared for us in heaven, and He called His people to come and eat and enjoy! But most often, caught up in their own little dramas, they ignored His call. So, in the person of His Son, Jesus, He "scooted down low" and became one of us. He gets our attention, meets us eye to eye, takes us by the hand and leads us to the feast.

Are you distracted by a dozen playthings of this life today? Turn around. He's there, waiting to meet you eye to eye. Supper's on the table, and all He wants is the pleasure of your company.

Take His hand, child. Trust Him. Then follow the Savior to the feast of God's goodness and enjoy!

> *I will fear no evil, for you are with me;*
> *… You prepare a table before me.*

PSALM 23:4–5

An Uninvited Gift

– Cynthia Spell –

God never wastes our valleys.

Marge Caldwell

Have you ever struggled with feeling angry with God when painful things happen?

Women come in different shapes and sizes, and from many backgrounds. But we all have one thing in common. Suffering is the common denominator we share. The difference in each of us is how we choose to journey through our hard places.

I used to get annoyed when people quoted Romans 8:28 to me in the middle of trauma. "And we know that in all things God works for the good of those who love Him."

Did I believe this to be true? Of course. But amid chaos and pain, I used to see nothing good. I felt angry and abandoned. I'd cry out, "Where are You, God? If You love us so much, why won't You stop the pain?" It's been a long process, but through the disabilities of my precious daughter, God has taught me to see great value in suffering.

For as long as I can remember, "Liquid Sonshine" has

been my nickname for my youngest, Mary Camille. Mary just naturally lights up a room when she walks in. She exudes joy, and as her faith in Christ matures, it's more and more evident she radiates God's love.

At twenty-three years old, Mary Camille has been through more heartache and suffering than most sixty-year-olds. At age fourteen she became ill with strep throat and mononucleosis. When the dizziness and fainting started, it was clear something was wrong, but it took five months before the diagnosis of postural orthostatic tachycardia syndrome (POTS) was made. At fifteen, she fainted and fell backward, crushing her lower-right occipital nerve. That's when her devastating head ticks and convulsions began.

Thankfully, there was no cognitive impairment from the brain injury, but the long-term result was nerve damage that causes migraines, chronic fatigue, and extreme noise sensitivity. At times she loses her ability to speak.

I'm thankful we couldn't see into the future. We would have lost heart if we had known that eight years later, I would still be her caregiver, and she would only leave home for doctor appointments and therapies.

Looking back, we see it as a journey God used to deepen our faith. I recently asked Mary Camille, "What do you think has been the most valuable part of your illness?"

She responded, "Although this journey has been painful and I'm certainly ready for it to end, I wouldn't trade what I've learned and who I've become through the suffering."

She paused for a moment and reflected, then added, "There have been a lot of losses that seemed big at the time. I can honestly say that not experiencing high school and college the way most people do could be the best thing that happened to me."

She continued, "I would have tried to fit in with the crowd, which could have led to big problems. I wouldn't have developed such a deep love for God and His Word. I wouldn't have such a close relationship with you, Momma. I wouldn't depend on God the way I do now. Even though it's hard, I believe the Lord is shaping me into the woman He wants me to be."

Looking deeply into the eyes of my daughter, I asked, "How do you keep from getting depressed?"

She responded with wisdom beyond her years. "I've learned that I can't dwell on what I didn't get to do. If I get stuck looking back and feeling sad, I'll miss the joy of today. I think God gave me a temperament that can handle this situation. I'm not angry with God. I've had to realize that He is still in control and say, 'I don't like this, I don't understand this. But I can't do anything to fix this.' It's up to God, and He will do what He wants with my life. I can trust Him. I cling to God because, at the end of the day, that's the most steadfast hope I have."

Mary Camille's conclusion? "All I can say is God has given me the peace that passes understanding. Of course, I want to be well so I can make friends, go to church, be in ministry, and get married. But for today, I just focus on the joy of what I *do* have."

My daughter and I have learned that suffering is a mysterious gift that produces dependency on God. It's certainly not a gift most people would sign up to receive. But as we have discovered, there are lessons of faith God can only teach us in the valley. We have tasted the sweetness of knowing God—and *that* is worth the price.

> For momentary, light affliction is producing
> for us an eternal weight of glory
> far beyond all comparison.
>
> 2 CORINTHIANS 4:17 NASB

A Little Bit of Wonderful

– Cathy Gallagher –

*A moment's insight is sometimes
worth a life's experience.*

Oliver Wendell Holmes Sr.

As my friend Rosie and I climbed to our seats in the steepest, highest section at the Van Andel Arena in Grand Rapids, Michigan, I hoped the evening would bring a little bit of encouragement into my depressing circumstances. But I didn't know I would experience an insightful moment and discover the answer to the question I had been wrestling with for weeks: *What do I do now?*

I was between jobs yet again, going through my third unwanted career transition in eighteen months. I felt sad, angry, dejected, and worried that employers would view me as un-hirable because of a dismal employment record. Attending the concert with Rosie was a pleasant break from the drudgery of job hunting, which hadn't been going well. I'd lost my last position on the heels of an economic downturn, and corporate America wasn't doing much hiring.

As we settled into our seats, Rosie and I joked about

our bird's-eye view of the stage and main floor far below us. Then the concert began. Memories of delightful moments from my youth filled my mind as Neil Diamond sang songs that had captured my teenage heart several decades earlier.

Usually at such events I looked out at the stage from a main-floor seat. Tonight, I was intrigued by how different the activity on stage appeared from high above rather than down below.

The intricate, perfectly timed movements of everyone and everything involved in the concert were fascinating to watch. Musicians took their places at precise moments. Props were placed on the stage and removed with seamless precision. The multicolored lights created a kaleidoscope of patterns dancing around the arena. Neil Diamond's movements were synchronized to the beat of his music.

Toward the end of the concert, a baby grand piano was raised onto the stage directly below us. Rosie nudged me and whispered. "Oh, Cathy, Neil's going to play!"

From my high-rise view, I watched Neil Diamond slowly approach the piano and lovingly stroke its exquisite wood-grain top. Reverently he said, "Look at this beautiful piano. Some people see a piano as an inanimate object, but I see it as an explosion of potential because of all the songs yet to be written on it."

It was an insightful moment. I didn't hear any of the remaining songs, too busy thinking about what Neil Diamond's statement stirred up in me. I remembered the

Bible says God created people in His image (Genesis 1:27), and now I saw myself as God sees me—as His explosion of potential because of all the untapped skills and talents inside me waiting to be released and used in a new job. The one I hadn't found yet.

Wow! I thought. Unemployment was like that piano—filled with limitless potential. What I did between jobs mattered. I could choose to keep my potential locked inside of me by worrying, complaining, and bad-mouthing my abilities and circumstances. Or I could choose to release my potential by embracing the opportunities unemployment contained. Opportunities such as the time to look for a job and the freedom to accept interviews without having to ask for a day off work!

Not only did I have a bird's-eye view of the concert; we had a "God's eye" glimpse of how differently circumstances look from where He sits, high above us, looking down from heaven.

I had been looking at my joblessness from a ground-floor view, seeing personal and professional failure and limitations. God, however, was looking at my potential and at everything He created me to become. He could see what I couldn't—how my past experiences and present job-hunting efforts connected to my future.

Suddenly I knew what to do. I needed to rise above my limited view and embrace God's broader view. I needed to put "a little bit of wonderful" into every day by treating my unplanned job loss as a springboard for unlocking my un-tapped potential as He opened new doors of opportunity. I needed to get up every day with hope in my heart because every day was an explosion of job-hunting potential, and only God knew which day would be *the* day I landed the right job.

When I left the concert, I didn't know I would spend the next six months reminding myself: *this could be the day I find a job*. Nor could I see that the door God eventually opened would be right where I spent so much time searching—Michigan's unemployment office. I guess He felt I'd spent so much time there, I might as well get paid for it. I also didn't know God would plant the desire in my heart to develop a Bible study for the unemployed, one that would put hope back into the hearts of others enduring my kind of discouragement.

Even though my future was uncertain as I left the concert, I felt like a new woman. I was no longer sad, angry, worried, and dejected. I was filled with hope and determi-nation. I had experienced how God's ways of looking at my life are higher and better than anything I imagined. And that felt *wonderful*.

"My thoughts are nothing like your thoughts," says the LORD.
"And my ways are far beyond anything you could imagine.
For just as the heavens are higher than the earth,
so my ways are higher than your ways
and my thoughts higher than your thoughts."

ISAIAH 55:8–9 NLT

The Crooked Tooth

— Shari Minke —

The great beautifier is a contented heart and a happy outlook.

Gayelord Hauser

"I can fix that crooked tooth for you," the dentist said.

Humph! I wanted to punch him in the nose! Never having met the man before, since this was the first time I had ever been to his office, I was offended that he didn't introduce himself before offering his comment. He didn't say, "Hello, how are you?" He simply pointed out my lack of perfection!

I surprised my normally shy self by bristling back, "Or ... we'll just leave it alone."

The insensitive man proceeded to pick up my left hand. Upon seeing my wedding ring, he retorted, "Okay. I see you already have your man."

I was crushed! I wanted to scream at him, *No, I don't!* My husband had left me a few months earlier. I wore the ring in hopes of his return.

The dentist's words haunted me. I interpreted them to mean, "Lady, with a crooked tooth like that, you were lucky to get *any* man!" I sobbed all the way home.

Years went by, and God brought another man into my life. He wasn't deterred from marrying me due to my crooked tooth. God used this gentleman to love me and nurture gifts hidden within me.

Time passed. I was teaching an adult Bible class at my church, and one of the men in the class was an orthodontist. He approached me after church one Sunday and spoke verbatim the words I had heard fifteen years earlier, "I can fix that crooked tooth for you." This kind soul had no way of knowing what a trigger his words were to my psyche. I disguised my reminder of an old hurt by chuckling and changing the subject.

A couple weeks later, I heard the words from the orthodontist *again*: "I can fix that crooked tooth for you."

While riding home, I had a bad attitude. I spouted off to my husband, "If he wants to fix my crooked tooth, then *he* can pay for it!"

On the following Sunday the orthodontist approached me. "I can fix that crooked tooth for you, and it won't cost you a red cent." As I recognized the sincerity in his offer, guilt washed over me for my previous unkind thoughts.

"Wow!" I responded. "That is very generous. Let me think about it."

On the ride home my husband said, "You can get your tooth straightened if you want, but as far as I'm concerned your teeth are fine."

I decided to survey those closest to me. Their responses intrigued me.

My teenage sons: "We never noticed that you had a crooked tooth."

My oldest daughter: "I have crooked teeth. Will he fix mine for free?"

My youngest daughter responded vehemently. "No! You can't get your tooth fixed. That's what makes you Mommy. That's your 'Mommy' tooth." When she was younger, she had named one of my teeth the "Queen tooth." It took me a little while to figure out she was referring to the gold *crown* on my back molar! She couldn't remember what it was called, but she knew it had something to do with royalty.

My parents liked my crooked tooth.

My prayer partner, Cindy, said, "I don't think I would like it if you got it fixed. It would make you look different. It just wouldn't be *you*."

My buddy Jan responded, "You travel around doing comedy characters. They are all imperfect people. I can't imagine any of your 'characters' having straight teeth."

The clincher came when my friend Vickie offered a challenge. "None of us is perfect. If you got your tooth fixed, what would you want to fix next?"

The next Sunday I gratefully declined the orthodontist's offer. His response surprised me. "Years ago I had a lady working in my office who had a tooth that looked almost identical to yours. I offered to fix her tooth, but she declined too. She stopped working for me, and I didn't see her for several years. One day I ran into her and noticed she had gotten her tooth fixed. You know what? I didn't like it! It wasn't *her*." We both laughed.

It's been freeing to know the quality of my life is not wrapped up in my physical appearance. In fact, I've decided to *embrace* my crooked tooth—but I do hope people will tell me when I have broccoli stuck in it!

GOD judges persons differently than humans do.
Men and women look at the face;
GOD looks into the heart.

I SAMUEL 16:7 MSG

Cleaning Up Our Act

– Lynn D. Morrissey –

Grace is love that cares and stoops and rescues.

John Stott

One thing I especially love about my dear friend Jo is that she's always poised for adventure. Over the years we've explored gourmet cooking, painting, and numerous other projects and passions. Though all our intentions have been good, some have fallen flat. Our closet shelves are depositories for unknitted yarn, unused exercise equipment, and unread books.

But rather than let failure defeat us, we lovingly prod each other to keep trying. The pièce de résistance was our home organization phase. This time we were determined to complete *something*. Analyzing the reason for our past derailments, we realized we had never developed a viable plan for success.

With each other's help, we would clean up our act.

One Saturday, despite being knee-deep in obligatory end-of-the-week housework, Jo and I cleverly escaped in the name of a good cause and met early at our favorite bookstore. There we purchased every home organization, house cleaning, and time management book known to womankind. We made a day of it and had a wonderful time. For hours we sat in the bookstore café (over breakfast, lunch, and finally dinner), reading, note-taking, and orchestrating a detailed strategy for deep-cleaning our houses. We were dauntless in laying out a battle plan that would have put General Sherman to shame. Finally, we had declared a war on clutter, with a surefire blueprint to win. There was no stopping us!

Over eight hours later, exhausted, I invited Jo to my house to share our game plan with my husband, Michael. Though he is always incredibly patient and understanding, I still didn't relish going home alone, knowing I'd left the house in complete chaos. True friend that she is, Jo was willing to face the music with me.

When Jo and I opened the front door and walked inside, we were amazed. The house was spotless! The carpets were vacuumed, the furniture polished, the clutter cleared. From stem to stern, everything was immaculate, shining, and orderly. My home organization dream had materialized without my even lifting a finger!

"Hey, Jo, this is miraculous! Just *reading* those books worked," I exclaimed, laughing.

Hearing our giggling, Michael appeared with his hands on his hips and a smile spreading across his face. "You know, ladies, at first I was skeptical about your organizational crusade. I thought that *doing* might accomplish more than *talking*. But in the end, I was proven wrong. You two met *long* enough for me to organize the entire house!" Amazingly, Michael even offered to help Jo with a few odd jobs when she was ready to tackle her house.

Jo and I have talked about this incident many times since, realizing that though we extended grace to each other, never criticizing our false starts or even our failures, it was my husband, Michael, who was the real grace giver. In a gracious gesture of generosity, he cleaned and organized our house—a job I had considered mine. I thought I had to develop a perfect plan before I could begin. Instead, though I didn't deserve it, Michael rescued me and did the job I had found impossible to accomplish on my own.

With great gratitude I also realized that I do not have to work hard to "clean up my act" or to perfectly understand the deep theological implications of salvation before receiving God's gift of grace. He loves me just as I am. He loves me so much that He stoops down when I am helpless and rescues me from a life of uncleanness. God, the ultimate grace-giver, sent His Son, Jesus, to die for my sins to make me clean and set me free. What I could never finish on my own, God finished for me through the death and resurrection of His Son. There is no more perfect act than that!

For it is by grace you have been saved,
through faith—and this is not from yourselves,
it is the gift of God—not by works,
so that no one can boast.

EPHESIANS 2:8–9

My Favorite Aunt
– Carol Kent –

A well-developed sense of humor is
the pole that adds balance to your
steps as you walk the tightrope of life.

William A. Ward

Aunt Delia was special. She never missed my birthday—and she always put cash inside the card. I also liked her because she married one of my mom's brothers, Uncle Jake. When the two of them came to visit, my siblings and I knew we were about to enjoy a laugh-out-loud visit with two very entertaining people.

My aunt was the "straight man," but her eyes always twinkled as she pretended to be the reasonable and serious part of this comedy duo. Uncle Jake was a hilarious story-teller. He was balding, and his hair formed a semicircle that surrounded his head like a misplaced halo. He kept a few hairs long so they could be combed directly across his bald spot. (I recently read that you know a man is in midlife crisis when he begins wearing his sideburns on top of his head.)

We never knew if Uncle Jake's stories were fact or fiction—and we didn't care. He told stories with dynamic body language and a full range of vocal inflection. During those splendid reunions, we begged him to repeat our favorite scenario. I remember sitting at his feet, waiting for little laugh lines to form around his sparkling eyes as he mesmerized us with our favorite wild tale. It goes like this.

One day when Aunt Delia, who we lovingly referred to as "Aunt Deal," left the house for work, she had a little extra time and decided to run a quick errand at the local shopping plaza. As she carefully backed out of the driveway, she felt an unnerving *thump, thump*. Her tires had run over something.

Aunt Deal stopped the vehicle abruptly and jumped out to discover she had just run over the family cat. Their limp, lifeless cat had met with an untimely death—and my aunt was distraught. Some animals are a friendly nuisance. But this animal was like a member of the family.

She knew her children would be devastated if they found their pet in this terminated condition when they returned home after school. Aunt Deal *couldn't* throw the cat in the garbage can. Not knowing what to do and wanting to show respect for such a valued pet, she decided to delay the decision until she could talk to Uncle Jake about how to tell the children and how to give the cat a proper burial. She grabbed a shopping bag out of the kitchen, placed the dead cat in the bag, and put the bag on the seat.

By the time she reached the shopping mall, the temperature had escalated. The parking lot was nearly full. She finally found a spot near the end of a long line of cars. Knowing that the rising temperature would cause the cat to stink, she placed the bag on the hood of the car where it would be in the open air while she dashed into the store for a few items.

When she emerged from the store, a woman was standing next to her car. The woman looked nervously to her right and then to her left, grabbed the shopping bag, and began walking briskly in the direction of the stores.

I can't miss this! Aunt Deal thought. She followed the woman, who passed three storefronts before checking out her "find." As she reached into the bottom of the bag, the expression on her face changed from glee to horror. Realizing the fur her fingers touched was a dead cat, the woman keeled over.

An onlooker yelled, "This woman's fainted! Call an ambulance!"

Within a short time, the rescue team arrived. The emergency workers laid the still-unconscious woman out on the stretcher. After they worked over her feverishly, they rolled the stretcher into the back of the ambulance. Someone in the crowd yelled, "That bag is hers!" so one of the rescue workers placed the bag on the woman's belly. The doors closed, and with sirens blaring, they drove off.

Uncle Jake never told us what the woman did when she

woke up and saw the bag, but we were all convinced that if she lived, she never stole again! Aunt Deal, complete with her deadpan straight-man facial expression, denied the incident ever happened. Uncle Jake, with that knowing, mischievous twinkle in his eye, insisted it did.

I still believe him.

Years later I realized what my favorite aunt taught me.

- Have fun with your spouse.
- Celebrate with your family members.
- Never stop laughing at life's crazy twists and turns.
- Hang out with your nieces and nephews.
- Put a little cash in children's birthday cards.
- Be willing to laugh at yourself.
- Everything in life is more fun if you develop a good sense of humor.

A cheerful heart brings a smile to your face;
a sad heart makes it hard to get through the day.

PROVERBS 15:13 MSG

A Graceful Skid

— Vicki Tiede —

*Life should not be a journey to the grave with
the intention of arriving safely in a pretty and
well-preserved body, but rather to skid in broadside in
a cloud of smoke, thoroughly used up, totally worn out,
and loudly proclaiming "Wow! What a ride!"*

Hunter S. Thompson

Laurie loved to hop on her Harley and ride down the road with the wind in her face and her responsibilities at her back. She worked full-time and had been a single mom for sixteen years to her two daughters. In the last year she had celebrated a reunion with the twenty-six-year-old son she placed for adoption as a baby. More recently she had taken a stand against alcohol and its grip on her life.

Riding her bike, however, was just for her. Laurie reveled in the opportunity to enjoy God's handiwork from behind the handlebars of her Harley while He whispered to her heart and the wind rushed in her ears.

On a stunningly beautiful July day, Laurie returned from a week-long vacation in the northern part of Minnesota.

For the past several summers, she and her girls had enjoyed vacationing at the same cabin. This year her girls had to work, so she made the trip alone on her motorcycle. Lounging by the lake with her Bible, journal, and a pile of books had been treasured time. She relished the hours spent alone with Jesus as He assured her of His faithfulness and abundant grace. With His promises freshly planted in her heart, Laurie returned home to see what new things God was about to reveal.

It was early afternoon when Laurie rode down a two-lane street that alternately passed through neighborhoods and businesses on her way to wash her motorcycle. Coming upon an intersection, she was momentarily distracted by the unusual number of cars in the left lane as well as cars parked on the street to her right. Turning her attention back to the road, horror struck her heart. A minivan had stopped to make a turn, and Laurie hadn't seen it in time. Now it was too late, and she was only a few feet from crashing into the back of the van.

She braced herself for the impact.

As Laurie lay in the hospital, she assessed the damages. Her left wrist had sustained a compound fracture and was now secured in a neon pink cast following two surgeries to piece it together with plates and screws. Her right wrist, also broken, sported screws and a clumsy, thick plaster cast. As a medical office administrator, Laurie had a career that depended on the use of these hands. To top it off, her hip, pelvis, and tailbone were broken in six places. Was God playing a cruel joke on her?

"Time," the doctors told her. "Time and complete bed rest will heal these bones." Laurie faced three months on her back and at least two additional months of rehabilitation in an assisted living facility. Concern for her girls, bills that needed to be paid, and missed work added additional weight to her burden.

Laurie had every reason to wallow in self-pity and depression and to cry out to God with questions and demands. She could have said, *Haven't I been through enough? I've done so much and I'm tired now. I am going to continue to follow you, but I really need a break!*

As I stood next to Laurie's hospital bed, I shook my head. Words escaped me. Laurie accurately interpreted my sense of helplessness. Then her mouth tipped up at the corners. "Hey, guess what!" she said. "I know that following Jesus doesn't come with the guarantee of a spotless driving record, which ends when I ride my Harley into heaven. I just thank God for graciously sparing my life. Because He protected my un-helmeted head, I've been given another chance to enjoy this life journey. I didn't do a thing to earn or deserve that!"

Laurie knew that while her bike was totaled, her life was not. Laying my hand on her cheek, one of the few places that didn't hurt, I smiled back. "Friend, God's love for you is simply more unimaginable than your circumstances."

Laurie's main concern was not the devastation of her current state of affairs. With God's grace, she was determined to enjoy the ride.

*Trust in the L*ORD *with all your heart*
and lean not on your own understanding;
in all your ways submit to him,
and he will make your paths straight.

PROVERBS 3:5–6

The Coat of Many Streaks
— Pauline Afman —

*It is one of the blessings of
old friends that you can afford
to be stupid with them.*

Ralph Waldo Emerson

Money has never been overly abundant at our house. Over the years, my husband has pastored in small churches. Although his paycheck seemed stretched to the max, we always made it to the next week and never went hungry. Since we had six children, hand-me-downs were welcomed.

A friend knew I needed a winter coat. One day she invited me over to let me know she had just the coat for me. It had belonged to her mother, who had passed away fifteen years earlier. Holding the coat tenderly, she spoke softly. "I couldn't bring myself to part with it before, but I know *you* will appreciate it. Mother only wore it a couple of times."

The coat looked somewhat promising at first glance. But when I tried it on, I discovered a few problems. After so many years in the closet, its age showed. The lining, which at one time must have been blue, now displayed faded purple streaks. It was tight across the chest and the sleeves were too short, but she thought it looked fine and was so pleased I would be wearing it. I knew if I rejected the coat, I would somehow devalue the love and generosity with which it was given.

I thanked her sincerely and took the coat home. But I never felt comfortable in it and dreaded each time I had to wear it. My feelings were conflicted because I had always taught my children to be thankful to the Lord for any used clothing that came our way.

Being in the ministry, I tried not to complain about things I didn't like and couldn't change. I only confided about it to my close friend Karen. I knew she would not repeat a word. When I unloaded my true feelings, she listened and understood.

Fall arrived and it was getting chilly, but I procrastinated when it came to getting out the coat. When it got so cold I *had* to, I went to the closet, and it wasn't there! I looked through all the closets in the house and decided I must have left it at church. It wasn't there either. I told Karen, and she again sympathized with me. "Don't worry about it," she said. "I'm going to take you shopping for a new coat."

Karen purchased a beautiful winter coat for me that year—one that really fit. A gift of love from a friend who cared. I occasionally thought about the missing coat but was relieved not to have to wear it anymore. Since I had worn the original hand-me-down for one season, it must have appeased the friend who originally gave it to me. She never mentioned it again.

A few years passed, and my husband accepted a call from another church. I was torn; I knew it was what God wanted, but the thought of leaving my dear friend Karen was difficult. She and another friend took me out for a special goodbye dinner at one of our favorite restaurants. The meal was delicious, but what came next was even better.

With a twinkle in her eye Karen said, "Pauline, we have a special gift for you. We want you to know how much we love you."

The gift was wrapped in a *huge* box, and I couldn't imagine what it could be. I was a little embarrassed at how much attention we were drawing. I carefully unwrapped the box, lifted the lid, pulled back the tissue paper, and then … *I screamed!* Restaurant patrons from every side turned to stare, but I was oblivious to the scene we were creating. You see, in the box lay the missing coat!

With much laughter Karen explained, "I took it, *knowing* I was going to buy you a new one. But I had a problem. I couldn't figure out what to do with it. I threw it in the garbage once, and then felt so guilty I retrieved it." We laughed until we cried.

As we left the restaurant, I told her, "Karen, I am *not* taking that coat home. You will have to dispose of it yourself."

Imagine my surprise when a few months after our move to a new city a letter from Karen arrived and a five-dollar bill fell out. Her note said, "Pauline, this belongs to you. Someone actually *bought* the coat at my garage sale!"

There has never been a time when God didn't come through when our family had a need. When it came to the coat, it wasn't so much a *need* as a *want*. God knew my heart and used my dear friend Karen to bless me.

A friend loves at all times.

PROVERBS 17:17

The Wilderness Experience

– Bonnie Afman Emmorey –

*Honor isn't about making the right choices.
It's about dealing with the consequences.*

Midori Koto

When Chris and her family moved away, I grieved. Our oldest sons were the same age, our husbands were close friends, and we had a very special friendship. Now she was a four-hour drive away, and I missed her greatly. We had no choice. Her husband's job was the determining factor. Phone calls kept us connected, but it wasn't the same.

The first summer after their move, Chris came up with a great idea—we would *vacation* together! She did the research and found a great house for us to rent on Lake Michigan near Sleeping Bear Dunes, a favorite place of both of our families. There was enough room in the house for both families, and we could enjoy quality time together.

We shared walks along the beach, roasted marshmallows over bonfires, swam in the crystal-clear lake, and played pinochle late into the night. A few days into our vacation, we made a day trip to one of our favorite sand dunes.

Standing at the base of the dune is an experience in itself—climbing it is another! With much laughter, we dragged and encouraged each other until we made it to the top. Once there, we decided to walk the three-mile trek up several more dunes to the Lake Michigan shoreline.

My sons, Nathan and Jordan, eleven and nine years old, and Chris's son Luke, also eleven, were off and running. Our athletic husbands had a hard time walking as slowly as us, and before long it was just Chris, Neil (Chris's four-year-old son), and me.

We passed other hikers making their way back to the starting point who assured us the hike was worth the trip. However, I saw surprise in their eyes when they caught sight of Neil. I knew they were thinking we were total *idiots* to be attempting such a feat with a young child. Chris and I took turns carrying Neil, and then we each took one of his hands, alternately swinging him between us and encouraging him to keep walking. Our enjoyment was only slightly dampened by the hot sun and our growing thirst. We were still busy catching up on months of being separated.

When we finally finished the three-mile hike and reached the shoreline, we were exhausted. We waded into the water and refreshed our hot, sweaty bodies. Before long, we were lying on the sand trying to gain strength for the return hike up and down the dunes to our point of origin.

My brain busily tried to figure out a shortcut. I could not see us making the trek back the same way we came. I shared my plan with Chris—our husbands could solve this problem! "Why don't we send Ron and Arny back to get the cars," I said, "and we'll just walk along this lovely shore until we reach a spot that has car access?"

Hesitantly, the guys agreed to our plan. Nathan, Jordan, and Luke thought it sounded like fun and decided to stick with us. Now we had a choice—north or south? It was a toss-up. None of us knew what either choice would bring. We walked south. Ron and Arny embarked on their walk to get the cars, and we began our adventure.

For the first hour Chris and I stayed together, enjoying conversation and the beauty around us. But before long, the three older boys took off and were outdistancing us significantly. Since the shoreline wove in and out with coves, I tried to keep the energetic boys in sight, but it meant leaving Chris and the lagging Neil behind. On our right was majestic Lake Michigan, and on our left tall cliffs. There was no choice but to keep walking.

We were completely unprepared. The sun beat down and we didn't have sunscreen. We had no food or water and resorted to drinking from the lake. Our small band of survivors stretched out, with Nathan leading the pack. The distance between each child grew. During the second hour we passed the monster dune, which went straight up 450 feet. People at the top yelled down with barely audible voices, incredulous that we were walking along the inaccessible shore. We kept walking.

At one point, I waited for Chris and Neil to catch up, thinking I could offer a word of encouragement. Chris looked at me with resignation and despair. "I know what Hagar and Ishmael felt like when they were sent into the wilderness to fend for themselves. Do you think we're going to make it?"

I didn't have an answer.

It took *seven* miles of shore walking before we had the first opportunity to go inland. Our worried husbands had been unsuccessful at finding anything closer. When they finally saw Nathan, Jordan, and Luke straggling along, they rejoiced and ran out to meet them. Chris and I were still a couple of coves away when Nathan raced back to us with renewed energy to say our wilderness experience was almost at an end.

When we finally met our husbands, we had walked a total of ten miles. The right sides of our bodies were scorched from the sun. Our feet were blistered from the sand. The children—including four-year-old Neil—required no recovery time at all. For them it had been a fun adventure. Meanwhile, Chris and I were simply thrilled to be alive!

It wasn't until later in the week that we were able to laugh about what happened. Checking a map, we discovered that, had we turned north instead of south, we would have only needed to walk one mile to reach a spot where we could be picked up. Oh, how we wished we had obtained a map ahead of time and made the *right* choice!

Our wilderness walk had spiritual application far beyond a vacation experience. As Christian women our map is God's Word, which needs to be consulted before important decisions are made. Not only was this a lesson *we* learned but it also became a talking point for an important family discussion.

> Show me your ways, Lord,
> teach me your paths.
>
> PSALM 25:4

Like a Mighty Wind

— Thelma Wells —

Several years ago I added something to my personal motto:
in Christ you can be the best of who you can be.
I use an acronym **"BEES."**

Be aware of who you are.
Eliminate the negatives.
Expect the best from yourself and everyone else and you'll be–
Successful.

Thelma Wells

I try to move through life taking God at His word, to praise Him in all circumstances, and to be stable in the storm—even storms with tornadoes.

Several years ago, my assistant, Pat Mays, and I were in downtown Nashville getting ready for a long evening's nap on the twenty-fifth floor of the Renaissance Hotel. Suddenly we heard what sounded like a locomotive trying to make its way into our room. It didn't take long to realize it was a tornado.

Remembering all those tornado safety drills from my

school days in Texas, I knew the bathroom was probably the most stable place to go for protection. With little time to think, I ran to the bathroom and huddled under the sink. To our horror, the building started swaying, sirens blared, and a frantic voice came over the intercom. "This is not a drill! We are having a tornado! Get to the ballroom now! Do not use the elevator!"

"We have to get out of here, Thelma," Pat said. "Now."

I didn't argue.

By the time Pat and I got to the eleventh floor, however, I could barely breathe from all the exertion. "I'm not going another floor," I said. "I'm going to die right here. You go on."

Pat had a "don't argue with me now" look in her eyes that implied, "I'm not leaving you, and you have no choice. Let's go."

After resting, I made it to the fifth floor. A couple of men, spying my obvious predicament, offered to carry me.

"You want to carry me?" I could not help but laugh. "Have you had children yet? You go on, so you can have your children. I'll get on by."

I finally made it, but I was the last one to arrive in the ballroom, and when I stumbled in, I headed straight for a chair and collapsed.

At last I caught my breath and looked around. Everyone was either on cell phones or trying to calm down. "I need a drink," said one guest. "I need a smoke," said another.

I soon joined in the chorus with "I need my Bible,"—

and yes, I had carried it with me on my journey downstairs.

With no scripture in mind, I opened my Bible to the fourth chapter of Mark—Jesus calming the storm on the Sea of Galilee. When I finished reading it aloud, I began to pray.

We later learned that a second funnel cloud headed for Nashville changed direction.

In Franklin, Tennessee, my fellow Women of Faith speaker Sheila Walsh heard on CNN that "people were praying in the Renaissance Hotel with their hands up." The next time I saw her, Sheila hugged me. Shaking her head she said in that lovely Scottish lilt of hers, "Thelma Wells, I knew it was you."

Counselors often say that circumstances and other people serve as "bumps" in our lives, bumping into the cup of our lives. Who we really are on the inside spills out in such moments. I can't always say that what spills out of me when I am bumped is what I would want Jesus to see. But on this night I was enormously pleased. When faced with a true crisis, and one tornado of a bump, what spilled out of me was faith and trust. Because this happened, others were calmed and encouraged, and Christ was glorified.

Fill up your cup with the Word of God today, and as you are bumped, what spills out will be life-giving to everyone around you.

I pray ... that you may be filled to the measure
of all the fullness of God. Now to him who is able to do
immeasurably more than all we ask or imagine, according
to his power that is at work within us, to him be glory.

EPHESIANS 3:17, 19–21

Yellow Ribbons

– Anne Denmark –

*Friendship without self-interest is one of
the rare and beautiful things in life.*

James Francis Byrnes

What were those patches of yellow on our trees? We could see them from a distance as my husband, Don, and I drove down the street toward our home. Closer now, we realized the whole yard was dotted yellow! As we pulled into the driveway, all four hundred large yellow bows came into view. They had decorated the cedars, the hedges, and even the trellises on the porch. From the balcony hung a huge banner with the words *Welcome Home*.

Don had just returned from a three-and-a-half-month mission at a refugee camp in famine-ravaged Ethiopia. His volunteer team brought medical aid to the orphaned, the sick, and the starving. Not having any medical training, I remained at home managing his medical practice, my business (a gift and book shop), and taking care of our three young children, ages eight, four, and two.

As our hearts rejoiced at this unexpected greeting, I

wondered who could be responsible for such an extravagant outburst of joy. It didn't take long to discover it was my dear friend Barb. As the brainchild of the whole production, she'd gone to the police department to find out where to obtain the thick yellow tape used to rope off designated areas. She acquired four large spools of it and headed to a local flower shop. There she shared her idea with the florist, Darcy, who immediately wanted to participate in the surprise. Barb explained to her, "I have this much money. Please make as many bows as you can." Four hundred beautiful bows later the spools were empty, and Darcy's wrists were numb, but the task was completed. Then Barb recruited additional friends to work like busy bees helping pollinate our front yard with fat yellow bows.

When I asked Barb whatever possessed her to do such a thing, she said, "I just *had* to do it. Don had been away so long, and you had waited many months for his return. When the idea came to me, I just had to."

Barb's gift was an unselfish act of love I still cherish. It would have been easier for her to feel twinges of jealousy. I had the large storybook home with the wraparound porches, the strong marriage, and the public respect as a doctor's wife. Barb worked long hours serving at the local tea shop, always desiring a fulfilling relationship with her husband. Yet her heart rejoiced with mine over my husband's return. And not just a quiet rejoicing—but with an extravagant outpouring of time and effort.

Several years later as Barb and I talked over coffee, I shared the difficult news of our family's coming move to Oklahoma. A painful, blank stare slowly filled her face. I searched for a way to soften the reality of our soon-to-come goodbyes. Then silence hushed our hearts, and misty eyes betrayed our deep understanding. We both knew our friendship would always remain, but we also knew it could never be quite the same. Distance and the passing of years would reshape our friendship.

Moving day arrived quickly. As we prepared to leave our hometown, many friends, including Barb and her husband, came to see us off. With this gathering of precious folks, we held hands in a huge circle and thanked God for friends and memories.

Three days later we pulled into an unfamiliar neighborhood, and there they were—those same yellow ribbons! This time they hung from oak trees and from the rafters above the entrance. The front door sported a sign that read, "Welcome Home!"

You guessed it! My buddy Barb had saved those bows all those years and shipped as many boxes of yellow ribbons as she could afford to our real estate agent in Oklahoma. When I called Barb to thank her for the yellow ribbon greeting, she said, "I know this move is so right for you, and I just wanted to welcome you home *again*."

What joy to my homesick heart to know friendship can travel the distance. Barb is a friend who only wants what's best for me. And the distance between her heart and mine is not really a long distance when measured in love.

Be happy with those who are happy,
and weep with those who weep.

ROMANS 12:15 NLT

Searching for Truth

– Cathy Gallagher –

The Lord is ever calling our wandering
thoughts and affections back to himself.

John Phillips

Oh, please, be home, I thought as I called my friend. I was eager to tell her about the book I had just read.

The phone rang, and memories of countless other calls I had made to Carol Kent over the years flooded my mind. I met Carol and her husband, Gene, twenty-one years earlier, and we became good friends. The pattern of those phone calls was always the same: I would blurt out, "Carol, you'll never guess what I've discovered."

Carol would say, "Tell me."

After I described the advice I discovered in the New Age book I had recently read, she would say, "Cathy, you are *such* a *seeker*."

I thought she was complimenting me. I wasn't ready to see what Carol knew and had tried to help me understand many times throughout the years—I was seeking lasting answers from temporary sources.

I read piles of books and listened to tons of recordings based on the movement that promised love and light, offering a foretaste of the coming era through personal transformation and healing. I also sought guidance from my weekly horoscope, assurance from fortune tellers, direction from my astrological chart, wisdom from tarot cards and numerologists, knowledge from psychics, and peace from Eastern Indian spiritual practices. The advice these sources offered never worked for long.

I was brought back to the present moment when Carol answered the phone. Our conversation began as usual: "Carol, you'll never guess what I've discovered."

"Tell me," she said hopefully.

"Do you remember my New Year's resolution to become fit by my fiftieth birthday by exercising and dieting because I thought life would be good if I looked good?"

She did.

"I went to the mall to buy an exercise outfit and a book to read on the gym's treadmill, noticed a Christian bookstore next to the sporting goods store, and decided to check it out. Seeing all the Bibles in different versions, colors, sizes, and price ranges overwhelmed me. I was about to bolt out the door when I thought: *The greatest book ever written is the Bible*.

"At the same time, one Bible caught my eye. I pulled it off the shelf, opened it, and read a verse and the note telling me how the verse applied to me. Then I bought it."

"Cathy, you bought a *Bible*? Did you *read* it?" Carol asked with excitement in her voice.

"Of course I did—cover to cover. Then I remembered how, when I was sixteen, I had asked Jesus into my heart to be the Lord and leader of my life. I was embarrassed that I'd relied on those New Age teachings all those years, so I prayed, asked God's forgiveness, and recommitted my life to Jesus."

"Oh, Cathy, Gene and I have prayed for twenty-one years that you would find Jesus! I was beginning to wonder if you ever would," Carol admitted. "What did you do with all of your New Age books and recordings?"

"I threw it all away—four boxes' worth! I still can't believe how much money and time I wasted on that stuff."

Before saying goodbye, Carol and I praised God for changing my physical fitness goal into a spiritual fitness goal, thanked God for answering her prayer of twenty-one years, and rejoiced that, at almost fifty, I had sought and found Jesus, the only source of lasting answers and advice.

Create in me a clean heart, O God.
Renew a loyal spirit within me.
Restore to me the joy of your salvation,
and make me willing to obey you.

PSALM 51:10, 12 NLT

Bubble Gum Kiss

– Karen Coy –

God diligently trails after us without hurrying us.
His voice speaks to us ... letting us know that apart from
Him we will never be complete. ... He does not just say,
"I love you," He constantly shows us how much.

Jan Johnson

I sat in the hot tub with tears streaming down my face. Blindly staring out the huge windows of my Colorado hotel, I hardly noticed the majestic mountain view. I desperately hoped anyone who walked by the glass enclosure would simply assume the chlorinated water had splashed my face. I had never felt more forsaken.

A year earlier, a relationship I had expected to end in marriage had simply ended. I spent the year trying to recover from the blow of watching the path I thought my life would take crumble before me. For a year I sat back and watched as, one by one, my friends set wedding dates. I hoped my pain wasn't evident while they excitedly shared their plans. Every day I mentally replayed angry tapes about grievances from my former relationship.

A year of unforgiveness. A year of unspeakable hurt.

I was still reeling from news I'd received right before I left on this business trip to Colorado. I had found out my former boyfriend was getting married. Quite frankly, I was angry. I was the one who was supposed to go off and live happily ever after—not him. It wasn't fair! To make matters worse, every area of my life seemed rocky. I was having financial problems, and my career path seemed uncertain. I felt like I was careening down the highway of life and God had most definitely fallen asleep at the wheel.

Despite my bleak outlook, I didn't want to ruin the weekend I had tacked on to my trip. In an attempt to salvage the day, I forced myself to go to the resort town of Breckenridge and arrived in the middle of their Memorial Day parade. Watching the floats go by filled with giggling children waving at their proud parents, I felt more alone than ever. As candy was happily tossed to spectators, the kids scrambled after the bubble gum and sweets.

Suddenly I realized how badly I wanted one of those pieces of bubble gum. But since it involved getting down on my hands and knees and knocking children aside, I resisted the impulse. But the desire wouldn't go away. "This is ridiculous," I chided myself. "You are a grown woman. Forget about the stupid gum." Feeling silly at this unprecedented obsession for bubble gum, I finally had to admit defeat. The parade ended, and there I stood empty-handed.

Slowly I made my way back to my car, which was parked

in the lot where the parade floats were returning. My hand was on the door handle when I heard a voice across the parking lot. "Hey, lady!"

I whipped my head around to see a boy of about twelve waving wildly from one of the floats. I turned to see who the "lady" was, but no one else was in sight. He was talking to me.

"Hey, lady!" he shouted again. "Do you want a piece of bubble gum?"

I stood there absolutely dumbfounded. Slowly I nodded my head and managed to squeak out a "Yeah!" In what seemed like slow motion, the boy wound his arm back and lobbed that piece of gum seventy-five feet in my direction. I am no baseball player, but I reached up and plucked that candy out of the air like I was born to catch.

Staring at the piece of bubble gum in my palm as if it were a precious treasure, I smiled. This might simply be the happy ending to one woman's quest for bubble gum. But I knew in my heart it was so much more. I could almost hear God's voice saying, "Karen, I haven't fallen asleep at the wheel. I know your needs—even something as small as a piece of bubble gum. And if I care about your smallest needs, think how much more I care about the big ones."

As I unwrapped the gum and popped it in my mouth, I felt God gently reassuring me that He was in control. In His time, He would provide everything I needed.

That was ten years ago. I'm now happily married to a

wonderful man, but I still have that bubble gum wrapper. Each time I come across it, I'm tempted to throw it away. After all, do I really need a piece of crumpled paper to tell me God cares about every hair on my head? But the truth is, sometimes I *do* need this tangible reminder. And so, each time I rediscover the treasured wrapper, I smile and think of the day God gave me a "bubble gum kiss."

"Therefore I tell you, do not worry about your life, what you will eat or drink; or about your body, what you will wear. Is not life more than food, and the body more than clothes? Look at the birds of the air; they do not sow or reap or store away in barns, and yet your heavenly Father feeds them. Are you not much more valuable than they?"

MATTHEW 6:25–26

Holding God's Hand in the Dark

— Thelma Wells —

Take the first step in faith. You don't have to
see the whole staircase, just take the first step.

Martin Luther King Jr.

As a scared little seven-year-old girl, I would sit in a narrow, dark, musty closet for hours at a time. But in those long, frightening hours when my downright mean grandmother confined me to "keep me out of her way," I still had my Jesus. I'd sing the hymns I'd learned at church, and when I didn't know the words, I would even make them up and just keep going: "Jesus loves me, this I know, for the Bible tells me so. Little ones to Him belong; they are weak, but He is strong ...."

Today I speak to thousands of women locked in the closet of their own pain. Women struggle every day with some hurt or another. I know this because I've been there. In many ways, I am *still there* because, frankly, life never lets up on this side of heaven. It's always something.

Like a mama longs to comfort her children, I want to gather all these wounded women in my audiences in my arms and rock them and sing lullabies of God's love to their wounded hearts—to embrace them with words of His comfort and hope.

But sometimes, girlfriends, real love has to be tough. And often the most loving thing I can do is get in the face of somebody stuck on the floor of despair and tell them like it is. And this is how it is: If you don't have the life that you have dreamed of, honey, you better learn to love the life you've got.

It all starts with an attitude of gratitude.

Even when life is not what we hoped, we can concentrate on the *good* things and what we *can* do. If we can walk and talk and see and smell and touch and taste—that's enough to keep us saying thank you to the Lord all day long.

I don't care if you're ill—you have something to be grateful for. You're still breathin', right? Thank God for the life you still have in the midst of your pain. While you're lyin' on your back, send praise songs and prayers to the ceiling and beyond—until your spirit breaks through to places where your physical body can't go anyway! (When praises go up, blessings come down.)

You've lost a loved one, you say, and now you can't find your way? Sweetheart, I say this in love: You are not the *first* and you will not be the *last* to walk through the valley of grief. Can you move your arms and legs? Can you cry tears and wipe them away and love someone else who is hurting too? Thank the Lord for the grieving process, for the new awareness of life's fragility and how precious we are to one another. Tell someone you love them. Your job on earth ain't over till it's *over*.

Lost your job? Unless you live in a foreign country, you are not starving. In this country, if you can flip burgers you can work. In America, when you're in trouble you can have a roof over your head and something to eat. You can find resources to help from any number of churches, good people, public libraries, and charitable organizations. Help is usually as close as a telephone call. Say a prayer of thanks and invite God to join in the adventure of meeting your family's needs.

Somebody has betrayed you, you say? Welcome to a part of the universal human experience. Sometime, somewhere, we will all feel betrayed. So what? Count the friends who *haven't* betrayed you, cling to the God who never leaves you, and be thankful for all that is right and beautiful in your life.

Think on those things that are good and beautiful and virtuous and true, and when you do, even though the problems are there, you have strength enough to deal with them and get through them. Embrace life. Laugh! Brighten the world with the twinkle in your eyes and the smile on your lips. Speak aloud words of gratitude: for your family, for your God, for the brilliant colors in tonight's sunset, for a plate of hot, flaky, homemade biscuits. (I was once asked, "What's your favorite food, Thelma?" I quickly answered,

"Anything that isn't tied down." So I could fill a praise notebook by simply listing the good foods I'm thankful to enjoy!)

When the world grows dreary and you are weary, come to the Lord like a seven-year-old little girl. Aren't we all really about seven years old on the inside anyway? Then begin singing the simplest of affirming songs. "Jesus loves me, this I know ...."

Trust me on this, girlfriend. Ain't no closet so dark that His peace cannot invade it and light you up on the inside.

This is the message we have heard from
him and declare to you: God is light;
in him there is no darkness at all.

1 JOHN 1:5

A Different Kind of Christmas

— Traci Ausborn —

*Sometimes the bravest and most important
thing you can do is just show up.*

Brené Brown

Things had been unusually hectic during the holiday season. I was working as a supervisor, and twenty-eight direct reports looked to me for a multitude of answers. As a charitable organization, we had extra projects going in addition to our day-to-day work and way too many deadlines. If we didn't accomplish our tasks, some families wouldn't have much of a Christmas.

Living with rheumatoid arthritis, I was totally familiar with pain and fatigue. But one cold December morning I awoke to something entirely different—red marks on my hands and an intense burning. The same agonizing pain stung my spine and from my shoulders to my elbows too.

It was a weekend, so I toughed it out until Monday, when I could get in touch with my rheumatologist. By then the red marks had turned to blisters—and if you've ever had shingles, you know the pain I refer to.

"Yep, it's shingles. Sorry," our staff registered nurse said.

"Great," I said through gritted teeth. "I can't do this now. I have too much to get done before Christmas."

Laughing, she shook her head. "Not sure you have a choice. Maybe this intense physical challenge is telling you to slow down."

On top of everything else, my husband's mother was scheduled to come visit. We always looked forward to her time with us, and really, all I wanted for Christmas was to have my family together and enjoy the "perfect" celebration.

My son and his wife had been married for a couple of years, so I was still getting used to the whole empty-nest thing. They would be with us at least one day over the holiday, and I wanted everything to be just right—the perfect gifts, the perfect meals, the perfectly decorated tree. All of which took time, energy, and strength. Things now in short supply. Even the smallest movements felt like torture.

Several days later, I was cleared to be at the office. "You are safe to be around," the nurse told me, "just keep your hands bandaged and your arms covered." And I did. But very soon I had a small understanding of how the lepers in the Bible must have felt. I was the recipient of uninformed comments that weren't meant to wound—but that did.

We made sure my mother-in-law had the most up-to-date information regarding my condition. Christmas wasn't far off now, and she needed to get her travel arrangements figured out. My daughter-in-law and I decided to do some last-minute shopping, with a stop at Starbucks on our agenda. We grabbed our coffees and were sitting in the car when my cell phone rang. It was Mom. I hoped she was updating me on her travel plans. I was always happy to hear her voice. She and I had become very close over the years, and she continues to be one of my biggest fans.

"I'm not going to come this year," she said quietly. I was heartbroken. Honestly, this wasn't a surprise, and I certainly couldn't blame her. Even though shingles isn't catching, the virus that causes the disease *is* contagious and can spread through direct contact with the fluid in blisters. Shingles is zero fun, and I'd been told that the older we are the worse it feels. Which was hard to imagine.

I was saddened by her decision, but I understood. "Are you okay?" I asked. A good question to ask since she was almost four hours away by car.

"Yes. I'm fine, but disappointed. I wanted to see you all."

"I understand. You have to do what's best for you."

In the passenger seat, my daughter-in-law listened quietly. When I hung up and rested my gloved hand on the gear shift, tears streamed down my face. Sadness, frustration, pain, and fear all circled overhead, but I hadn't decided which one I was experiencing most intensely.

I'd messed up the perfect Christmas. I truly felt like one of the lepers of old. And just as this thought crossed my mind, my daughter-in-law put her hand on mine and said words I have never forgotten. "I'm not afraid of you."

God blessed me abundantly with a daughter-in-law who loves and trusts the Lord. Her words were like a salve over all the wounds of the past month—physical, mental, emotional, and even the ones I caused myself.

It was a different kind of Christmas—but it was beautiful and blessed. I learned that perfection isn't all it's cracked up to be. Somehow everything got done in time for the special day. And the precious bonus was a growing, even more precious relationship with my daughter-in-law.

Gracious words are a honeycomb,
sweet to the soul and healing to the bones.

PROVERBS 16:24

The Royal Coffers

– Jeanne Zornes –

In the greatest difficulties, in the heaviest trials, in the
deepest poverty and necessities, He has never failed me; but,
because I was enabled by His grace to trust in Him, He has always
appeared for my help. I delight in speaking well of His Name.

George Muller

"Mail for you," I told my high school daughter when I
picked her up after school on a cloudy December day. In
half a year she'd graduate, and college decisions weighed
heavily on us.

"Probably another 'I'm sorry, but' letter," she said, wig-
gling her thumb through the seal of the envelope. The
sender was a university to which she had applied for a high-
stakes scholarship.

I held my breath, afraid to hear the news. I'd debated
about bringing the envelope. Should I have left it on her
bed so she'd get the bad news in private?

A few months earlier, we'd entered the parenting era of
college bills. Her older brother started junior college, where
scholarships covered all his tuition. But he'd have to finish

his engineering degree elsewhere. And for our daughter's violin studies, she too would need to go elsewhere—but where? How?

Two in college on a teacher's pension was an impossible equation. Retirement rules had pushed their dad out of his thirty-one-year job. Now he substitute taught for less than half his former wage while I worked out of our home and provided care for his elderly mother. Giving to God's work still came first. We shopped garage sales, clipped coupons, and did without. We lived in a small tract home and drove older cars. The kids and I substituted on newspaper delivery routes for "fun money."

While I tried to be content, a corner of my heart resented the constant financial pressure. With greater expenses ahead, I'd asked the Lord, "How are we going to do it?"

At first I'd seen hope glittering for our daughter in the possibility of her being chosen queen for our community's big spring festival. Along with the rhinestone crown came a substantial scholarship. But that Cinderella dream had a price: two hundred appearances at a grueling pace, including scores of parades out of town. My daughter saw clearly how this might jeopardize her dreams of graduating with a hard-earned 4.0 GPA, serving as golf team captain, and playing her violin concerto in the spring concert.

Though I told her I'd respect her decision, I'd pushed, thinking I was helping God work it out. She wrestled over taking on more commitments with her life already too full—despite the scholarship at stake. She became increasingly moody and uncertain as she prayed. Finally came the day of decision. To compete, she would need to attend a mandatory meeting after school.

Doubts churned inside me. *What would she decide? What was God's will?* Tears streaked her cheeks. "I can't do it," she said. "It's just not me."

So instead, we returned to applying for general scholarships, hoping something else would come through. My daughter's principal nominated her for a prestigious full ride at a state university. Out of hundreds of top-notch nominees, only twenty-five in the state would be chosen, based on academics and leadership. But she'd never held a student body office. Her chances of winning seemed as remote as landing on Pluto.

Now here she was in the car, two weeks after her decision to skip the royalty competition, holding the official-looking envelope from that university.

"Here comes another disappointment," she muttered. As I pulled out of my parking space, she pulled out the letter. "Mom! I got it—*the full ride*! Tuition and housing—renewable all four years with a 3.5 GPA!"

Suddenly I became a distracted driver! I could only say, "Praise God!"—over and over.

Three months later, our son won generous tuition scholarships to the same university. His housing bills still loomed, but God had spoken. We could trust Him to provide the rest from the royal coffers of heaven, however He worked it out.

Living simply for the Lord had been simpler when life wasn't so expensive. But God used the stretch of lean finances to remind me that He excels at financial planning. When He disposed of *my* solutions, He had something much better. He'd supplied our need and bolstered my faith.

Who needs a rhinestone crown when your Father is heaven's King?

*We humans keep brainstorming options
and plans, but God's purpose prevails.*

PROVERBS 19:21 MSG

Sisters of the Heart
– Carol Kent –

Joy is a net of love by which you can catch souls.
Mother Teresa

The invitation was unexpected. I had been asked to travel to Frankfurt, Germany, to speak for the five-day Worship and Study Conference sponsored by the Protestant Women of the Chapel. The group was comprised of more than five hundred military wives and some active-duty military women from American bases all over Europe. After landing in Frankfurt, my husband and I were driven to a picturesque ski resort town where the event was being held in a lovely hotel.

There was excitement in the air. I was immediately struck by the strong sense of sisterhood these women had. Most were in their twenties or early thirties. For many, this was their first time living away from home in a foreign country, far from their mothers and biological sisters. Many had husbands deployed in Bosnia or Kosovo, and they felt alone in an unfamiliar environment—*except for the presence of their military sisters*. They explained to me that when you are in the military, you get close to each other very quickly because you get moved often—frequently every two years—and there is a strong bonding with other women in like circumstances.

My assignment was to speak every morning for the keynote sessions during the conference, and I also led a workshop on sharing your faith. When I came to the part about praying the prayer to become a Christian, I noticed several blank stares. "Perhaps some of you have never invited Jesus to be your Savior and you would like to make that choice today." That day *seven* young military wives prayed and became Christians.

The following day as I walked down the hall toward my hotel room, I heard a voice behind me calling. "Carol, Heather wants to become a Christian, but we're not sure we can remember all the words of that prayer. Can you come help us explain how she can ask Jesus into her life?"

I pivoted on my heel and followed my new friend down the hall. When we got to the hotel room, a group of women were already gathered, eager to see Heather become a Christian. Heather had long brunette hair, and it appeared she had not had much sleep. She smoked with vigor as if the tension of this situation was causing her stress.

I said, "Why don't we begin by having some of you share how you became Christians."

A lovely young woman next to me immediately put her hand in the air. "I'll go first. I went to church my whole life, and I have always been a very good person. It wasn't until I came to this conference that I found out you have to make it personal. I just became a Christian one hour ago!"

I fought back tears. The one-hour-old believer had given the first testimony. One by one the rest of the women shared with honesty what their lives had been like before Christ and the difference He made since they came to know Him personally. It was a holy moment, and a hush fell on the room.

After a pause, I said to Heather, "You've heard some pretty amazing stories today. It's very simple, but sometimes people make it complicated. The Bible teaches that God sent His Son, Jesus, to this earth. He was sinless and perfect. He grew to maturity and began His public teaching ministry at the age of thirty. The religious leaders of the day didn't recognize Him as the Savior of the world. They mocked and ridiculed Him. At age thirty-three, He went through the most painful death invented by mankind—death by crucifixion. Jesus hung on a cross and paid the price for all the wrongdoing in the world—my sin and yours. But the story didn't end there. He rose again, and He's in heaven today preparing a place for those who believe."

I concluded, "Heather, I don't think it was an accident that you were invited to this conference. God knew you needed to find Him in the middle of all that's happening in your life. Are you interested in following me in a prayer to invite Christ into your life right now?"

Heather took one final drag on her cigarette and vigorously nodded her head. We all stood in a circle, and this sisterhood of military women looped their arms around each other. With no embarrassment or hesitation, Heather began to pray out loud, confessing her sin and inviting Jesus Christ to be her Savior and Lord.

There were no dry eyes. As the prayer ended, Susan, the woman who had invited Heather to the conference, embraced her friend and gently rocked her back and forth while singing a song of welcome into the body of Christ.

I hugged Heather and Susan and asked, "How did the two of you meet?"

Susan smiled. "We both have daughters named Harley."

I found myself chuckling, thinking only motorcycle people would name a baby girl Harley. But God had a different idea. The story unfolded. I learned that Heather and Susan were in the military commissary at the same time when Susan called her daughter, "Harley!" Heather wondered who was calling *her* daughter, and the two women met. But they had *nothing* in common. Susan was deeply involved in her faith, and Heather wasn't interested.

Time passed and God put it on Susan's heart to invite Heather to the conference. Heather's husband had been deployed, and she was lonely and fearful. The love and concern Susan displayed drew Heather to accept the invitation. And that's how two military wives became sisters in Christ at a hotel in Germany.

God didn't go to all the trouble of sending his Son merely to point an accusing finger, telling the world how bad it was. He came to help, to put the world right again. Anyone who trusts in him is acquitted.

JOHN 3:17–18 MSG

Can Anything Good Happen at 5:30 a.m. in the Airport?

– Lucinda Secrest McDowell –

When God closes a door, he often opens a window.

Anonymous

I couldn't have been more discouraged professionally. As I packed my hotel room to leave the Christian Booksellers Convention in California, I wept and wailed at God.

"I give up. This writing stuff is way too hard. No one likes my ideas anyway. If I quit now, all my unwritten books won't even be missed!"

My current book project had been circulating through several publishing houses to no avail. And now a literary agent who met with me said, "No one wants this book, Cindy. No one will publish it, and no one will buy it."

Still, I refused to accept the futility and finality of her statement. I clung to the idea that my book on wisdom shared by women turning fifty was a needed and positive way to encourage my own generation of aging females.

Through my sobs I went to God in prayer. "Lord, please

show me your path for my writing career. I'm willing to give it all up, but I'm also willing to persevere. Which will it be? You are in control, and I submit to your will. Amen."

It seemed I had barely cried myself to sleep when the alarm rang at five o'clock the next morning for my shuttle to the airport. Upon arrival, I wandered through security and to my gate while looking, I'm sure, like the failure I felt myself to be.

I sat down in the waiting room with some authors of fiction, and we began to chat about the convention. Soon another woman joined us and introduced herself as an editor for a Colorado publisher. Our consensus was that we were all eager to get home to our families. When the loudspeaker announced boarding flights, everyone stood up to disperse to various gates.

Turning to the editor, Mary, I said, "Well, now that you're leaving the convention, is there one manuscript you had hoped to acquire but didn't?"

"As a matter of fact, there is," she replied. "My boss really wants a book on women turning fifty."

My jaw dropped open. In the few seconds we had before boarding, I briefly explained my book proposal and asked if I could send it to her.

"You bet!" Mary replied.

My long cross-country flight was filled with new hope—not just the hope that this fifth book might finally find a home but a renewed confidence that God was still guiding each step and ordering my paths, even as I tentatively approached my own half-century mark.

This year, four million people turned fifty, and I was one of them. What have I learned so far? What truths will continue to guide and sustain me in the rest of life's journey? Well, at least one of them is that God is in control, and He will open and close doors at will. All He asks is for us to relinquish control and step out in faith and obedience.

I love the Lord, because He has heard
My voice and my supplications.
Because He has inclined His ear to me,
Therefore I will call upon Him as long as I live.

PSALM 116:1–2 NKJV

When I Had Everything

— Allison L. Shaw —

*Friendship improves happiness and abates misery by
the doubling of our joy and the dividing of our grief.*

Cicero

When I was a little girl, I hoped and wished and prayed for
a sister, but I never got one. My mom told me that sometimes we have to adopt our sisters along the way. And so
throughout my life, God has blessed me with some relationships that have transcended friendship to reveal a bond
of sisterhood in Christ. Theresa belongs in that category.

I met Theresa after she and her husband, Jeremy, moved
to Sacramento from South Carolina. As a transplant to
California myself, we shared the immediate bond of being
far from home. When Theresa revealed she was struggling
in her marriage, I volunteered to meet with her weekly for
prayer and accountability. I thought I was being a good
friend. She needed me. Little did I know how much I
would need her.

Within weeks of initiating our Monday evening accountability time, my husband, Michael, and I came under

spiritual attack. We had some financial difficulty, Michael sprained his ankle, our car was stolen, and our apartment was robbed. Theresa was on her knees in prayer with me every step of the way. Often our friends see us at our best, for girls' nights or celebrations, but Theresa loved me when I was at my worst.

During my quiet time with the Lord one evening, I came across the stories in 1 Samuel that chronicle the friendship between David and Jonathan. It's a story I was very familiar with, but it read differently this time around. It occurred to me that King Saul's son, Jonathan *should* have been the next king of Israel. Yet even when David was anointed king and promised everything that was rightfully Jonathan's, Jonathan still risked his life for David. It was such a vivid portrayal of friendship. I wondered if I could be that selfless for a friend.

When I told Theresa I was expecting my first baby, she was ecstatic! For weeks we had prayed that we would be pregnant at the same time so we could share the joys of motherhood together. What made her joy that much more precious was that Theresa had been trying to have a child for over a year with no success. I was amazed at her outpouring of love and excitement. As she jumped up and down, shrieking with glee for me, I realized that Theresa was just like Jonathan. Even when I was granted everything she had ever desired, Theresa willingly laid aside her own sorrow to share in my happiness. She could have been angry, jealous, or resentful, but instead Theresa was selfless—a living example of Christ's love.

A few weeks later, Michael and I lost our precious baby, and it was Theresa who came to sit with me while I was overcome with grief. She brought flowers, bagels, cream cheese, and tea. She made me laugh when my heart was broken. But more importantly, she loved me with the love of a sister in Christ. All of those evenings on our knees before the throne of God, interceding for one another's burdens and praising the Father for our joys, had knit us together in a bond that transcended friendship.

Theresa says that before leaving South Carolina, she specifically prayed for a friend who would be an accountability partner, a prayer warrior, and a sister in Christ. Theresa's prayers were answered, and I am the one who was blessed.

Friends love through all kinds of weather,
and families stick together in all kinds of trouble.

PROVERBS 17:17 MSG

The Friendship Factor

— Diana Pintar —

An older sister is a friend and defender–
a listener, conspirator, a counselor,
and a sharer of delights. And sorrows, too.

Pam Brown

"Who's going to the hospital with you?" my friend Cindy caringly asked.

"It's just a simple test," I said. "No big deal."

It *was* a big deal. The truth was, I was terrified. Something had gone horribly wrong with my swallow. I had forgotten how to do it. After several horrific choking episodes, I knew I had to act.

The scheduled test was a videofluoroscopy, a video X-ray that shows what is happening during a swallow. I was afraid I would either choke or have to expel unswallowed food (a polite way to say *spit*) during the test.

What might I blurt out under stress? I certainly did not want witnesses to *that*!

"I'll be fine, Cindy," I said, in what I hoped sounded like a "subject-closed" manner.

"I'm going!" she stated emphatically.

I relented, realizing I needed a good friend to make it through this dreaded experience. "Okay."

Cindy enthused, "We'll make a party out of it!"

A party! Only Cindy could turn a videofluoroscopy into a party. Every woman needs an encourager like Cindy.

Cindy began to plan our party with an essential concern. "What are you wearing?"

I grinned. "A hospital gown, I suspect."

"Oh, right!" Cindy paused and then blurted, "Let's run over to Victoria's Secret and try to find you some awesome underwear!"

"I don't think so, Cindy," I protested.

She countered. "We *have* to dress you up in some way!" She thought a moment. "How about a crown?"

I sat in stunned silence. Images ran through my mind of "glamorous me," parading through the hospital in the standard-issue, backless hospital gown—with a crown upon my head. A smile was born deep in my heart. It wound its way up to my face, erasing every trace of fear. I laughed out loud.

"It sounds crazy." I exclaimed. "But Cindy, *crazy* is exactly what I need right now!"

As the day approached, word of our "videofluoroscopy party" spread. Sandee, another friend who is a part of my circle of Christian sisters, asked if she could join us. A third friend, Beth, decorated my crown with a Scripture verse,

"I can do all things through Christ who strengthens me" (Philippians 4:13 NKJV).

When the big day arrived, I sat waiting for my "chauffeurs" to arrive. My eyes fell on two helium balloons. They were remnants of the birthday I celebrated earlier that week.

If I'm wearing a crown, I decided while gathering the balloons, my friends are carrying these!

Upon arrival, my friends presented me with a delightfully tacky dollar-store crown made of plastic, complete with big, garish, fake rhinestones. We paraded into the hospital, my entourage and me. I walked a bit ahead of them. Chin high, crown atop my head, I waved at startled onlookers, doing my best Miss America imitation. Cindy and Sandee walked a few steps behind, carrying the birthday balloons.

"What are you celebrating?" startled spectators inquired.

"Life!" we chortled.

I donned my gown and stored my clothes—all but my crown. When I emerged from the dressing room gowned, crowned, and ready to go, I was greeted by my giggling girl-friends—both of whom were attired in hospital gowns of their own.

Joy is contagious. Others joined our celebration. The waiting room resounded with laughter and happy noise.

When our party pals were called for their X-rays, they protested! Cindy, Sandee, and I bid them adieu like old friends. "Goodbye! Goodbye! God bless!" we called after them as they left for their tests.

Then it was my turn.

"Diana Pintar?" the technician said as she rounded the corner, chart in hand.

"That's me!"

She surveyed the scene, then read aloud the card that decorated my crown: "I can do all things through Christ who strengthens me." She smiled—a very big smile.

I am a woman of faith. The technician's smile indicated that she was one of my Christian sisters too. I was greatly comforted by this realization.

The test began. I stood in the tiny X-ray room. Cindy, Sandee, and our new friend, the X-ray technician, stood in a small, glass-enclosed booth across the room.

"Let's start with the cracker on the right." The technician's instructions came through a speaker in the corner.

I felt alone. Fear returned. With shaking hands, I picked up the cracker. I tried. I failed. Hot tears flooded my eyes and began to wet my cheeks.

"This isn't working!" I protested.

"Diana," the technician called out, "remember what it says on your crown? 'I can do all things through Christ who strengthens me.'"

In the window, I could see Cindy, Sandee, and the technician. They were all smiling at me. Cindy and Sandee waved and clapped their hands. The X-ray technician gave me the thumbs-up sign.

Suddenly it did not matter if I passed or failed the test.

This had been an amazing, joy-filled day! These women were more than friends; they were my sisters in Christ. Their support turned what could have been a devastating experience into one of my most delightful memories.

It's better to have a partner than go it alone.
Share the work, share the wealth.
And if one falls down, the other helps, ...
By yourself you're unprotected.
With a friend you can face the worst.
Can you round up a third?
A three-stranded rope isn't easily snapped.

ECCLESIASTES 4:9–12 MSG

Pass It On

— Thelma Wells —

We turn not older with the years,
but newer every day.

Emily Dickinson

At sixty-one years of age, I began to realize my years left on earth needed to be used in a way that would multiply what God has given me, in ways that would be lasting and in hearts that would go on when God called me home. I prayed about it and waited as God, in His own creative ways, continued to affirm how I was to do this. In fact, three times, someone said to me, "Thelma, I believe God wants you to share the wisdom you've gleaned with other women in leadership ministry who will be faithful to pass it on." The third time I heard it, I cried and cried. I had no choice, even with my busy schedule, but to obey.

So I have taken on a nurturing, loving, and instructing role for sixty-five women through a ministry I call the "Daughters of Zion."

My formal title in this new endeavor is a "Mother of Zion," but these African American women of various ages from all phases of ministry—no matter how seasoned—call me Mama T. These sharp, strong women have been called by God to be everything from evangelists, teachers, and preachers to pastor's wives and praise dancers. Two of them, I'm privileged to say, are my own grown daughters.

The group began meeting once a month at my home for a ten-month program. We talk about relationships, unity, time management, health, and healing a broken heart, as well as other issues. Never one to do anything halfway, I got so excited about this new ministry I created notebooks, brochures, handouts, and even homework for my girls.

There are many questions, issues, struggles, or women's ministry questions they need to discuss with someone. This is true even if they've been ministering for years. "Who can I trust?" they ask. "Who can I talk to?"

I feel so privileged to be the mentor these women can trust—a friend with whom they can let down their hair and be real. One of my spiritual daughters, Priscilla Shirer, said, "I believe in the scripture that says the older women should teach the young women. I believe there are a lot of young women who think they know everything, and that is so far from the truth."

Cathy, another minister in our group, said, "All of us have the public face, but we have real concerns going on in our private lives."

In the time we've been meeting, I am seeing much fruit, and our time together is incredibly rich.

Has it been a balancing act to handle the new ministry and my other responsibilities?

Oh, girl, yes, yes, *yes*!

But do I wish I'd decided *not* to take on this assignment from God?

Oh, no.

I wouldn't trade this experience for anything. The grandmother in me loves mothering, loving, and caring for these ladies. It is natural for me, giving out of my area of giftedness. And I have learned in my years of walking with the Lord that what God has ordained you to do, He will sustain you to do.

Is there something God is calling you to do, but you are unsure if it is of Him? Be open, ask, pray. I typically ask my Father to confirm what He wants me to do at least three times, so I know I am hearing Him clearly, especially if the opportunity is going to require a long time commitment. But when He does affirm and you are sure in your heart that you're hearing His voice, relax and begin to follow Him one step at a time.

You may make some mistakes and have some challenges as you follow God. Expect that as part of the process. But I can assure you the pain you may feel as you step out in faith and follow His leading is nothing like the pain of regret, looking back and wondering, *What if . . .*

What if I had listened and obeyed? What might I have been? What might I have done?

Listen to God's voice to your heart, my friend, as He nudges you toward your place of greatest service and impact. Then follow with no looking back, no regrets. Finally, watch Him fill you up so that you can splash over to bless His children. There is no greater joy.

Whoever refreshes others will be refreshed.

PROVERBS 11:25

The Shopping Divas

– Bonnie Afman Emmorey –

*Sisters are girlfriends, rivals,
listening posts, shopping buddies,
confidantes, and so much more.*

Carol Saline

The Afman girls have many similarities—and one thing we all enjoy is shopping. My sister Jennie and I are probably the most alike in our technique. We both consider shopping our best sport, and we are competitive.

A few years ago, the two of us were in San Diego for a seminar, and we decided to stay an extra day so we could do some shopping in Tijuana, Mexico. We knew it would be an unusual escapade, but we had no idea just how much adventure awaited us the following day.

We started out bright and early as we mentally prepared for wheeling and dealing with the locals. Jennie and I jumped on a train near our hotel and got off when the conductor announced that we were at the border crossing. Then we faced our first problem. *We couldn't find Mexico!* We expected signs or at least something indicating we were coming to the end of one country and entering another. How could we "run to the border" if we couldn't even find it?

We must have looked bewildered because a man walked over and asked if we needed any help. We asked him to point us in the direction of the Mexican border, and he said, "Follow me. I'm going that way myself."

The man was *totally* dressed in black leather, with stringy, shoulder-length hair, and he was smoking something. This was not a guy I would feel comfortable following anywhere, certainly not into a foreign country. But before I could say a word, my sister sincerely thanked him, fell into step beside him, and struck up a conversation.

Knowing we had to stick together, I brought up the rear. We followed him down a walkway and through a turnstile. This was it! We were now in Mexico, he told us. There were no border guards or customs officials.

I tried to gently pry Jennie away from the fellow in black leather, but it was not working. I overheard him say, "How would you like to see the *real* Mexico?"

I was thinking, "Are you *kidding*?" But before I could protest, my sister responded with an affirmative word, and once again I couldn't leave her. So I simply followed along.

He took us to an old bus stuffed with people and their livestock. I felt like I'd walked onto the set of an old movie. My seat was next to a woman and her pig. I tried hard to lean *away* from the aroma. The air was so foul I could hardly breathe. I had visions of being abducted and sold into slavery and my husband and sons hearing about it on the evening news.

Jennie still conversed politely with her newfound friend and had even progressed to showing him pictures of her family. I shot visual warning daggers in her direction.

In spite of my fears, the man in black turned out to be a kind person who gave us excellent advice. He helped us get off at a bus stop in downtown Tijuana, suggested where we should go and where not to go, and gave us instructions regarding what to offer a cab driver for the ride back to the border.

That day two sisters made choices that could have landed them in serious trouble. However, in spite of our uncertain circumstances, Jennie and I enjoyed a glorious day of shopping. We perfected the art of bartering and bought sombreros and ponchos for our kids.

We seriously considered keeping the events of the day to ourselves—but decided it might be better to tell our families and use our impulsive actions as a lesson in what *not* to do. We knew God had spared us from potential danger and we should have sought wise counsel *before* entering a foreign country.

Without good direction, people lose their way;
the more wise counsel you follow, the better your chances.

PROVERBS 11:14 MSG

Bequest of Wings

– Cynthia Reynolds –

He ate and drank the precious words,
His spirit grew robust;
He knew no more that he was poor,
Nor that his frame was dust.
He danced along the dingy days
And this bequest of wings
Was but a book. What liberty
A loosened spirit brings!

Emily Dickinson

I peeked in my daughter Jessica's bedroom and found her curled up with a book. "What are you reading, sweetie?"

She looked up with a knowing smile. "*Anne of Green Gables.*" My heart swelled with joy, and I found unexpected tears in my eyes.

All of my pregnancies required an unwanted period of mandatory bed rest. When I was pregnant with Jessica, the doctor ordered *complete* bed rest, and I was terrified. Following two miscarriages, I wasn't taking any chances. I lay there tense and fretful, with thoughts swirling in my head:

Is it okay to walk to the bathroom? Should I lie flat, or can I raise my head a little?

A friend who called to cheer me up pointed out a simple truth. "You are doing all you can. Worrying won't help. In fact, it might do harm." I relaxed a little. My friend said, "Do you have a good supply of children's books?" I thought she was talking about the cloth books and the *Pat the Bunny* book I had acquired in anticipation of our little one's arrival. But before I could answer, she set me straight. "I'm talking about *Anne of Green Gables, Treasures in the Snow, Five Children and It*—children's books."

I had never heard of most of these books, even though I had been an avid reader when I was young. "No," I admitted.

"Well," she said, "send your husband to the library to get these books for a start. Now, do you have a pencil and paper?" I wrote furiously as she gave me the names of titles and authors.

When my husband got home, I greeted him warmly. Then I handed him the list as if it were a prescription and said, "Go. Go now. Please get me these books." I felt an urgency to have these books in my hands, as if reading them would be the best medicine.

And in a way, they were. When he returned home with the books, I plunged into reading. From that moment on, I never worried about my unstable pregnancy. I was absorbed in another world—immersed in Anne's heart-breaking childhood and tender optimism, captivated by

Annette's hard heart and the miraculous way it was softened, and enchanted by the children who found a sand fairy and learned that having your wishes granted is not something to take lightly.

God used the creative gifts of others to bless my heart, my mind, and ultimately, my body and the tiny person clinging tenuously to life inside my womb. He used the stories to captivate my imagination for noble purposes and steer it away from fear. Other books could have done as well, more adult books. However, the simple truths I was reminded of in these well-written classics calmed me, centered me, and filled me with hope and joy.

Now, ten years later, I stood at my daughter's door, watching her read one of the same books that comforted me when she was growing in my womb. "It's my favorite, Mom," she said with a smile.

God's care for us in such rich and meaningful ways was never more evident to me than in this moment.

Many times when a friend in need has asked for advice, I've handed them a book. "Start with this," I say, knowing it will bring God's deep and abiding comfort—perhaps for generations to come.

Whatever is true, whatever is honorable,
whatever is right, whatever is pure, whatever is lovely,
whatever is commendable, if there is any excellence and
if anything worthy of praise, think about these things.

PHILIPPIANS 4:8 NASB

Falling in Love

— Penny Williams —

*Unfulfilled plans are often pathways to God's greater purpose.
When our focus is on God's purpose over our plans,
we are freed from the pressure they create.*

Christina Patterson

I had been a single parent for eighteen years when someone unexpectedly entered my life. He was compassionate, intelligent, funny, and best of all, he made me feel like I was the most important person in his world. Though we lived a distance from each other, he would often make the trip after work to meet me for dinner. Evenings passed quickly as we shared the highlights of our day, our love for our families, and had discussions of shared spiritual values and principles that were important to us.

The months passed quickly, and our bond grew closer. One evening the phone rang. "Penny, could we attend my church tomorrow and then go to Bahama Breeze for dinner?"

Excitedly, I accepted. Tom attended a large, dynamic church we enjoyed being a part of, and the restaurant he chose was where we had our first date. During dinner the easy flow of conversation and laughter emphasized how well our relationship was developing and how compatible we were as a couple.

Tom pulled out a travel magazine. "Penny, if you could go anywhere in the world, where would you like to go?"

Puzzled, I tried to read what he was thinking. I stammered, "Tom, I don't understand." Taking my hand in his, he held it tenderly while looking deeply into my eyes. My heart pounded as he expressed his love for me and his desire to spend the rest of his life with me. Believing the most amazing dream had just come true, I accepted. The rest of the summer passed quickly as we made plans for the wedding and excitedly looked forward to sharing our lives together.

As fall approached, the time grew closer for me to resume my ministry schedule, which involved weekend travel. As I prepared to leave for the first conference, Tom expressed his reluctance about my going. I assured him I, too, was going to miss our time together but expressed the desire God placed in my heart for ministry. He teasingly responded, "I'll be the great-looking guy in the baggage claim area, waiting for a pickup." I smiled back at this sweet, gentle man I loved.

The first conference of the fall is always exciting, filled with lots of activity and time to catch up with staff members after the busy summer. This time, however, I found myself unusually restless. In the quiet of the night, I wrestled over my relationship with Tom. Not wanting to believe God was asking me to give up this relationship, I sought out the counsel of my close friend, the director of the conferences. Together we talked and prayed as I sorted through my relationship with Tom.

After making the return trip home, I walked the long corridor to the baggage claim area. Looking up, I saw Tom waiting. My heart leaped at the sight of him—then sank, knowing what I needed to do. However, it was late, so I chose to keep the conversation light.

The next night when he picked me up for dinner, Tom appeared deep in thought. Our usual animated conversation of shared experiences and dreams was reduced to a silent reluctance to talk until Tom said, "Penny, I missed having you here."

"Tom," I said, "I believe God has placed me in ministry."

"Penny, I need you to make a choice. I don't believe you can give the time necessary for a good marriage and be in ministry at the same time."

Sadly, I knew my dream with Tom was ending. I responded thoughtfully, knowing my heart belonged first to God. I had been internally wrestling with this issue for several weeks. A decision had to be made. It was hard for me to form the words. "Tom, God has placed me in ministry. I can't marry you."

A painful silence clouded the rest of our dinner and the ride home. Silently, Tom walked me to the door. For the first time since meeting, our words were strained and carefully chosen as we said our goodbyes.

I longed for the companionship and security Tom provided. I loved our dinners together and the lively conversation of our shared interests and future goals. But I realized I was in a relationship with a man who was not interested in having me pursue my dreams, and he did not support my passion for ministry activities. I'd had to choose between being God's woman or Tom's wife.

Today I'm still a single parent, and I'd still like to be married when the right man comes into my life. Until then, I am much happier knowing I sought godly wisdom from the Bible and from a trusted friend. I enjoy the work of my private counseling practice and the opportunity to pour my extra time into ministries furthering God's kingdom agenda.

It feels good. It feels right.

I will instruct you and teach you in the way you should go;
I will counsel you with my loving eye on you.

PSALM 32:8

Did You Know
My Neighbor, God?

– Carol Kent –

*Just remember that God is stronger than all
our missed opportunities and poor choices.
His plan for your life remains.*

Lessons from Home

Our son was nine when we moved into the house on
Lexington Drive. Our next-door neighbors, Olivia and
Lucas, had three children. Fun-loving and energetic, these
involved parents coached local hockey teams and had season tickets to the Michigan State University football games.
Olivia's contagious laugh could be heard a block away. She
loved life—and everybody knew it!

I liked Olivia from the first time I met her. Our back-
yards were divided by an invisible property line, and over
the next ten years we had numerous opportunities to
chat as we watered and weeded our gardens. I often wondered what Olivia's spiritual background was, but I didn't
want to be pushy. After all, we were neighbors. Once she

commented about seeing one of my books in an area bookstore. I wanted to be careful about coming on too strong about God. I often thought about inviting her to a women's event at my church, but the timing never seemed right. Both of our families were so busy.

Olivia loved roses. She had planted a large rose garden on the side of her house and was the neighborhood's rose expert. For her birthday, Olivia's brother constructed a picturesque brick walkway beside the roses and topped it off with an arched, white arbor. It looked like a fairyland—and it faced my family room window.

Mid-August came. Olivia and I hadn't seen much of each other. I was in my backyard watering flowers when she stepped outside to do the same. "Olivia," I yelled across the yard. "Your roses are more beautiful than ever."

"Well," she said, smiling, "our son is graduating from high school next spring, and I want the yard to be pretty for his open house. It's hard to believe the time flies by so quickly."

I was thinking the same thing. Time. It *did* move swiftly. We had lived next door for ten years, and although I had a very congenial relationship with my neighbor, I had never even invited her over for coffee—*in ten years*.

She smiled and waved as she turned and walked up the steps of her porch. I thought about inviting her to the outreach dinner the women in our church had planned, but I felt uneasy about bringing up the subject.

The following day was filled with answering correspondence, doing several batches of laundry, returning a few calls, and contacting family members about an upcoming reunion. Gene and I had a late dinner, watched a favorite show, and went to bed.

The next morning my doorbell rang. It was another neighbor. As I opened the door, Mary stuck her head inside. She was breathless. "Have you heard about Olivia?"

"No," I said. "Is something wrong?"

Mary's words ran together. "Yesterday she went to work as usual, and she had a severe headache. During the day the headache got worse, and her coworkers took her to the hospital. The pain didn't let up much, so they decided to keep her there overnight. Lucas was at the hospital with her last night and she said, 'Honey, the kids need you more than I do. You go home and I'll see you in the morning.'"

Tears glistened in Mary's eyes. She went on. "At four this morning she had an aneurysm, and the scan showed flat brain waves. They'll do another scan in twenty-four hours, but the prognosis doesn't look good."

Olivia never woke up. On Wednesday morning she was pronounced dead, and that evening doctors from university hospitals flew in to harvest her organs. On Friday afternoon I attended my neighbor's memorial service.

I always thought I would have a more perfect time to talk to her about matters of life and faith—but we were both so busy. And I put it off too long.

Be ready to speak up and tell anyone
who asks why you're living the way you are,
and always with the utmost courtesy.
Keep a clear conscience before God.

I PETER 3:15–16 MSG

One of God's Favorites

— Cheryl Gochnauer —

> If God had a refrigerator, your picture would be on it.
> If He had a wallet, your photo would be in it.
> He sends you flowers every spring and a
> sunrise every morning. ... Face it, friend.
> He is crazy about you!
>
> Max Lucado

On a rare outing alone following my double mastectomy, I was happy to see a parking spot relatively close to our local box store. But just as I was about to pull in, a black pickup truck zoomed up and dove into it.

Usually this makes me lose it. But I just didn't have the energy, and I continued up the row.

I couldn't believe it.

The disabled parking space closest to the door was open. No cars were in front of me or behind me or waiting with their turn signal on. Thanking God for being so nice, I pulled in. I hung my temporary tag, then sat for a few moments to gather myself. I could do this. It's good to push yourself a bit, get your body stronger, and help it heal.

Plus, I'd gone to all this trouble to put on makeup and wear something other than my bathrobe.

I maneuvered out of the car and started for the door. There were two women nearby, walking together toward the entrance.

Suddenly I overheard one of them speak with disgust: "I just *hate* those well-bodied people who steal parking spaces meant for disabled people who need them!" Verbal abuse, combined with a few choice cuss words spewed from two women who obviously had to park farther away than I did.

I kept walking, not willing to use up precious energy where it would do absolutely no good. Plus, I was kind of flattered to be considered "well-bodied," considering the surgery I'd been through recently.

Once inside, the first person I met was George. Tall, lanky, and at least seventy-five years old, he grinned and welcomed me. I grinned back, took a couple of steps, then turned around. "George, thank you for being so kind."

He said, "Well, now. I almost never hear anything like that. Usually it's just the opposite." I told him how badly I had been treated outside and asked who his supervisor was. I was going to make sure this person knew what a great employee the business had in George.

Beaming, George pointed the way.

The supervisor frowned when hearing about my parking lot encounter but loved that George had saved the day and promised to recognize him at the next group meeting.

Then I met Glenn (who I soon learned was eighty-one) in the juice aisle. Holding one of fifty-three varieties of V8 juice in his hand, he said, "All I want is plain tomato juice. Just tomato juice." I pointed out plain tomato juice on the top shelf. As he brought it down, he talked about how great it was for holding off diabetes and other maladies. He was so convincing, I decided to get a bottle.

"Would you mind grabbing it for me, Glenn? I just had surgery and can't reach up there."

He did, happy to help a youngster like me. "You're the lady those women were yelling at in the parking lot." I nodded. "What kind of surgery did you have?" I told him. "Well, you shoulda just lifted your shirt and showed 'em! That woulda shut their traps."

I smiled, realizing I had actually considered doing just that, and thanked Glenn for being so perceptive.

"You gonna be okay, honey? I mean, they got all the cancer?" When I assured him that they had and I just needed to heal now, he said, "Thank God or whatever higher being there is."

"His name is Jesus," I replied.

"Well, yeah. God or whoever."

"Jesus. Hey, Glenn—I'm loving talking with you, but my energy level is at about 12 percent, and I need to get my shopping done." He shook my hand and off I went.

As always happens at this store, the three things I needed turned into a cartload, and by the time I got to the registers I was pretty sure I wouldn't survive a wait in one of those lines.

"Come on over here," a young cashier said. "I'm just opening up and I'll take care of you."

I prayed silently. *Thank you again, God!*

As she scanned and bagged my items, I asked if carryout was available. "I'm right outside the door, in the first disabled parking space." No problem. She got on the intercom.

Nobody came. She spoke over the intercom again. Several employees sauntered by, all deaf.

An assistant manager, Lea, stepped up, asked what we needed and said she'd wheel my basket out herself. She started off briskly, then looked over her shoulder at my pitiful pace and slowed. "Sorry. You just take your time."

I swayed, standing by the open trunk as Lea loaded my bags. I told her the story, from the vicious women to friendly George, to the happy manager I'd spoken with, to Glenn in the juice aisle, to the young cashier and now, to her.

"Lea, I just don't have the energy to go back in the store and find your boss. But when this story comes up at the next group meeting, I want you to raise your hand and let them know you helped me too!" Agreeing, she shut the trunk, put away the cart and waved goodbye.

I rested in the car until recharged, then headed home, feeling absolutely great. I had just experienced another one of those awesome instances where God takes something spiteful and makes something good out of it. Sometimes

God reminds me that I am *seen*, I am *known*, and I am *loved*. I know He loves all of us equally—but there are certain days when I know I'm one of His favorites! And yes, His name is Jesus.

> Surely, LORD, you bless the righteous;
> you surround them with your favor as with a shield.

PSALM 5:12

Finishing Well

– Bonnie Afman Emmorey –

*If you want to finish well in the Christian life,
then live your life in obedience to the Lord.*

Anne Graham Lotz

Crocheting was one of my mother's special talents. She would often make a beautiful afghan for one of her six children as a reminder of a marker moment in their lives. I treasured each of the items I'd been given through the years because Mother did something special as she worked on each piece—she prayed for the person who would receive the gift.

When my sons were born, they each received a baby blanket made just for them filled with prayers for their future life choices—accepting Christ as their personal Savior, making wise decisions at school, saying yes to the right life partner, to name just a few.

When my firstborn son was about five, Mother made a full-sized afghan to go at the end of his bed for extra warmth on cold nights. It was beautiful and well used. I knew that prayers for Nathan were in every stitch of that blanket.

When Jordan turned five, I expected him to receive one as well. Time passed, and I finally resorted to asking if he would be getting one. Mother seemed distraught. She said, "Honey, I started it so many times and found that I am too stressed right now. It ended up with my stitches being all tight and uneven. I took it apart each time. I finally hired a friend to help me finish it."

Whaaat? *Someone else* was finishing my son's blanket? What about the prayers? But Mother was concerned with making sure it was finished well.

Time passed, and it wasn't until many years later that I realized what my precious mother had done. She needed help finishing the afghan, and she found someone who could assist her in doing it well. The fact that she'd probably prayed more for Jordan than for any of her other grandchildren during that time totally slipped past me, and her prayers were *not* undone with the stitches she pulled.

Finishing well became a bit of a mantra as Mother started to age. We became walking buddies almost every afternoon. She had always been on the plump side, but mother started to lose weight. I can still hear the phone ring with her voice at the other end saying, "Are we going to walk today?" The year she turned ninety-three she walked over two hundred miles and took joy in logging them on an app on her computer.

Winter came and she fell, breaking her hip. While some things changed, that momentary setback didn't stop her.

She faithfully did all the exercises prescribed by her physical therapist and slowly regained her ability to walk. We started our outdoor exercise carefully, but before long, my phone rang daily. Her cheery voice was on the other end asking if we were planning to walk.

On her ninety-sixth birthday, I had no ability to envision a world without Mother. She always battled back from any sickness, and I was oblivious to the fact that she would not be with me forever. She was once again walking regularly and took joy in her accomplishments.

November came and Mother caught pneumonia. As a family we celebrated Thanksgiving in the hospital, gathered around her bed, sharing our many reasons for praise. We sang our favorite hymn, *To God Be the Glory*. We held hands and prayed for Mother's healing.

Before long she was moved to a transitional health facility and started the long road to regaining her strength. I never doubted she would enjoy a full recovery and be back posting her miles in short order. But that did not happen.

One afternoon, my sister Joy and I were with Mother, and it had been a rough day. She wasn't feeling well, and congestive heart failure was causing her lungs to fill with fluid. She was tearful. I asked Joy to put on some praise music. Joy reached for Mother's iPad, and within seconds a worship team singing *Worthy Is the Lamb* filled the room with praise.

Instantly, Mother stopped weeping, and her low alto

voice joined the voices streaming from the device. Both of her arms shot up into the air. Joy grabbed one and I grabbed the other to allow her to keep them raised. She needed our help. We joined in the singing with tears streaming down our faces. She was praising God with her whole heart, and we were privileged to witness a God-filled moment. She was finishing well.

I have fought the good fight, I have
finished the race, I have kept the faith.

2 TIMOTHY 4:7

About Carol Kent, General Editor

Carol Kent is a best-selling author and international speaker. With vulnerable openness, irrepressible hope, restored joy, and a sense of humor, she directs you to choices based on God's truth. Carol says, "When God writes your story, you will be in for the adventure of a lifetime!"

Carol is Executive Director of the Speak Up Conference, a ministry committed to helping Christians develop their speaking and writing skills. She and her husband, Gene, founded the nonprofit organization Speak Up for Hope, which benefits inmates and their families.

She holds a master's degree in communication arts and a bachelor's degree in speech education. She is a former radio show cohost and has often been a guest on Focus on the Family and many other media outlets.

Carol has trained Christian speakers for over twenty-five years. She has been a featured speaker at Women of Faith, Extraordinary Women, and Women of Joy arena events. She is the author of over twenty-five books, including the bestselling *When I Lay My Isaac Down* and *Becoming a Woman of Influence* (NavPress), a 365 page-per-day devotional titled *He Walks with Me* (Christian Art Gifts), the 2021 Christian Market Christian Living Book of the Year, *Staying Power: Building a Stronger Marriage When Life Sends Its Worst* (Revell, coauthored with Gene Kent and Cindy and David Lambert), and *Life Lessons for Moms* (Christian Art Gifts).

She and Gene are both fans of tracking down the best cup of coffee in every city they visit. Their favorite activity is watching sunsets together.

Connect with Carol

www.facebook.com/AuthorCarolKent
www.X.com/CarolKentSpeaks
www.instagram.com/CarolKentSpeaks
www.CarolKent.org
www.SpeakUpMinistries.com
www.SpeakUpConference.com
www.SpeakUpforHope.org
For information, call 586.481.7661

About Thelma Wells

With upbeat, joyous enthusiasm Thelma Wells, popular author, international inspirational speaker, and businesswoman, spent her life offering heart-to-heart encouragement and assurances of God's personal intervention and direction to women everywhere she went. A speaker with Women of Faith, Thelma was President of A Woman of God Ministries and of Daughters of Zion Leadership Mentoring Program in Dallas. She was a professor at the Master's Divinity School in Evansville, Indiana. Her books include *The Buzz, Bumblebees Fly Anyway, God Will Make a Way, What's Going On Lord?* and *Girl, Have I Got News for You!*

As an African American woman, Thelma was instrumental in bringing racial diversity to the Women of Faith conferences. Through her ministry to thousands of women, Thelma believed she found the fulfillment of a desire God put in her heart and the culmination of a burning passion she had to share His love with women of all backgrounds.

Thelma was quick to point out there are more than 37,000 promises in the Bible. She was willing to share her own experiences of how Christ kept His promises to her, and she wasn't afraid to call on Him in prayer to fulfill His promises. Whether it was in her irrepressible spirit breaking through in her prayer life ("Am I supposed to keep asking you to do this, Sir?") or in a spellbinding vignette about a family member, Thelma's authentic passion for the Lord and faith in His love were ever present.

Thelma went home to be with the Lord not long ago. Her desire for her audiences and her readers was to help them discover God's promises. She reminded all of us that God will make a way! For additional information go to www.thelmawells.com.

Contributors

Charlotte Adelsperger was an author and speaker who wrote four books and material for more than two hundred publications. Published widely is her story "Between the Lines," first seen in *A Second Chicken Soup for the Woman's Soul*. Charlotte's poetry appears in magazines and gift books. She was passionate about speaking on the encouragement ministry.

Pauline Afman was a Bible teacher, a pastor's wife, and a woman of prayer. She was the mother of Carol Kent, four more daughters, and a son. A master storyteller, she entertained and encouraged her family and other audiences for much of her adult life. Pauline left us for heaven, but her stories still touch our lives.

Traci Ausborn has authored several nonfiction articles and is working on a Christian Mystery novel series. A former church business manager and pastoral secretary, she enjoys speaking at conferences and facilitating training sessions at the corporate level. She is a program manager for Providence Health & Services and makes her home in Camas, Washington. She enjoys spending time with her husband, son, daughter-in-law, three grandchildren, and her dog, Bandit.

Sandi Banks is a devotion writer for numerous publishing houses. She offers hope by pointing the reader to God and His Word. As a faculty member at Carol Kent's Speak Up Conferences, Sandi inspires others to experience the "Joy of Writing and Publishing Devotions." Please visit her website, a place where hope meets humor. sandibanks.com.

Melissa Sutter Brower dedicated thirty-five years to the field of education, where she found great joy in nurturing students—mind, body, and soul. She lives in Grant, Michigan, with her husband, who loves to take her on camping adventures. Her adult children and their spouses bring tremendous happiness to her heart.

Karen Coy is a former television producer living her dream of residing in a Victorian house in Grand Rapids, Michigan. She loves all things vintage and is passionate about creating beauty in her home and garden. She attends Ada Bible Church, serving on the worship team and mentor program.

Anne Denmark is a seasoned professional coach. She affirms the gifts in others and supports them in loving like Jesus. She has served as an instructor for Professional Christian Coaching Institute and as a faculty member of the Speak Up Conference with Carol Kent Ministries. Anne lives in Nashville, Tennessee with her husband, Don.

Jennie Afman Dimkoff is an author and international speaker for retreats, conferences, and for events on college campuses. She serves on the boards of Our Daily Bread Global Ministries and Speak Up for Hope. She is also on the faculty at the annual Speak Up Conference. JennieDimkoff.com.

Bonnie Afman Emmorey is conference director for the Speak Up Conference, a ministry that equips Christian speakers and writers. She's also the director of Speak Up for Hope, a prison ministry. Bonnie and her husband, Ron, have two grown sons, two awesome daughters-in-law, and six delightful grands. They reside in Wichita, Kansas.

Cathy Gallagher has been a marketing manager, salesperson, customer service representative, customer service director, assistant dean, and president of her own speaking and writing business. She has also authored articles for businesses and is published in *Guideposts* magazine.

Cheryl Gochnauer is founder of Homebodies, a ministry for at-home parents. She has written several family life books and more than a thousand print and online articles. Now retired, Cheryl still races for her laptop to document those precious "Did you see what God just did?" moments. Her children, Carrie and Garrett, are now grown, married to their soulmates, and both recently became first-time parents. In an epilogue only God could orchestrate, their babies, born several states apart, entered the world within hours of each other. Their grandmas laughed! You can reach her at cherylgo58@gmail.com.

Judy Hampton was a public speaker and Bible teacher who taught powerful principles with a touch of humor and an emphasis on the Word of God. She spoke internationally for women's conferences and authored the book *Under the Circumstances*. Judy has left her earth shackles for heaven, and she is greatly missed.

Gracie Malone has been published in a wide variety of magazines and is the author of several books, including *Off My Rocker: Grandparenting Ain't What It Used to Be*, *Still Making Waves: Creating a Splash in Midlife and Beyond*, and *Unafraid: 365 Days Without Fear*. Gracie hails from Grapevine, Texas, and she's known as a specialist on the topic of grandparenting.

Lucinda Secrest McDowell was passionate about helping people choose lives of serenity and strength. A seasoned mentor, she was the award-winning author of sixteen books, including *Soul Strong* and *Life-Giving Choices*. She's at home with her Lord now, but she loved to encourage young mamas, coach writers and speakers, and speak blessing over hungry souls.

Shari Minke believes with God *all* things are possible! He has transformed her from a shy, fear-filled person to a faith-filled speaker. Shari has a passion for encouraging others into a deeper walk with Jesus Christ. She and her husband, Tom, have four children and nine grandchildren.

Lynn D. Morrissey encourages transparency in Christ as a professional author, speaker, vocalist, certified journal facilitator (CJF), and founder of Sacred Journaling. She's the author of *Love Letters to God: Deeper Intimacy through Written Prayer*, other books, and a contributor to numerous bestsellers, magazines, and blogs. Lynn and her husband, Michael, have one grown daughter, Sheridan.

Diana Pintar is the past president of Next Step Ministries, Inc. She has been a women's ministries director and a national speaker. Diana was also on the faculty of Speak Up Ministries, equipping the next generation of Christian communicators. She loves discipling, coaching, and encouraging women to follow hard after God.

Cynthia Reynolds is a writer, artist, and spiritual director. She has a thriving art practice and leads prayer and writing retreats. She and her husband live in Madison, Wisconsin and visit their three grandchildren in Boston as often as they can. Contact her at wildberrymom@gmail.com.

Maggie Wallem Rowe is a national speaker and dramatist who writes from Peace Ridge, her home in the mountains of North Carolina. Maggie is the author of *This Life We Share* and *Life is Sweet, Y'all*. Visit her at MaggieRowe.com.

Rachel St. John-Gilbert is author of *Wake Up Laughing: Offbeat Devotions for the Unconventional Woman*.

Allison L. Shaw was a project specialist for ProjectAttain! a collective impact nonprofit that helped adults who have some college, but no credentials, complete their education. She is passionate about post-secondary education, curriculum development, and great books. Allison, Michael, and their three children are based in Nashville, Tennessee.

Ginger Shaw serves as President of California Against Slavery (californiaagainstslavery.org) as well as serving as chair of the Southern California Safe Shelter Collaborative (safesheltercollaborative.org) to locate shelter for survivors of abuse and exploitation. Experience as a Bible study leader, speaker, and college communications instructor has taught her about the power of story to reach people across all ages and cultures.

Cynthia Spell is a Christian counselor, keynote speaker, and the author of *Deceived by Shame, Desired by God*. Her heart's desire is to teach women this truth: there is nothing you've done that is beyond God's redemption. He can turn our brokenness into a beautiful mosaic masterpiece.

Vicki Tiede is an author, speaker, and owner of a health coaching business. As a champion of truth, hope, and health, she mentors and equips others to fulfill God's plan in their lives by stewarding their health. Vicki wrote *When Your Husband Is Addicted to Pornography: Healing Your Wounded Heart.*

Penny Williams is a psychologist. The emphasis of her practice is on biblically based Christian counseling for children, couples, families, and individuals. She also provides telehealth services through the Counseling Center of West Michigan, as well as providing evaluations and counseling to inmates through Michigan Department of Corrections.

Jeanne Zornes, of Washington state, has written *When I Prayed for Patience … God Let Me Have It*; *When I Got on the Highway to Heaven … I Didn't Expect Rocky Roads*; *When I Felt Like Ragweed God, Saw a Rose*; and *Spiritual Spandex for the Outstretched Soul.* Her weekly blog can be found at jeannezornes.blogspot.com.